MW01017160

# *Beyond Literacy*

## THE SECOND GUTENBERG REVOLUTION

R. PATTON HOWELL, EDITOR

Saybrook

Publishing Company, Inc.

San Francisco          Dallas          New York

Copyright © 1989 by the Mentor Society

All rights reserved. No part of this work may be reproduced or transmitted in any form, electronic or mechanical, including photocopying and retrieval system, except as may be expressly permitted by the 1976 Copyright Act or in writing from the publisher. To request permission write Saybrook Publishing Company, Inc., 5307 McCommas, Dallas, Texas 75206.

**Library of Congress Cataloging-in-Publication Data**

Beyond literacy : the second Gutenberg revolution /
    edited by R. Patton Howell.
            p. cm.
        ISBN 0-933071-32-9 : $7.95
    1. Books and reading--United States.  2. Literature-
-Appreciation--United States.  3. United States--Intellec-
tual life--20th century.  4. Literacy--United States.    I.
Howell, R. Patton, 1921- .
Z1003.2.B49  1990                      90-8425
028'.9'0973--dc20                      CIP


Cover design by Fred Huffman
Book design/Typography: Special Projects Group




**Saybrook Publishing Company, Inc.**
5307 McCommas, Dallas, Texas 75206

Printed in the United States of America

Distributed by W.W. Norton & Company
500 Fifth Avenue, New York, New York 10110

For my dear wife, Joan,
and my children and grandchildren . . .

# Acknowledgements

Most of the articles in this volume owe their origin to a 1988 meeting on the nature of reading held by the Mentor Society and Saybrook Institute in San Francisco. The meeting brought together the right people at the right place and the right time. Many thanks to those institutions.
Specifically I am honored to thank:

The Nobel Foundation for remarks by laureates Wole Soyinka 1986, Joseph Brodsky 1987, and Naguib Mahfouz 1988.

**Harper's Magazine** for its editor, Lewis Lapham's *On Reading*.

**Academic Technology** for Frederick Turner's adaptation from *Silicon Tools: Dreaming the New Academy*.

Cambridge University Press, New York, N.Y. for C. S. Lewis' **An Experiment in Criticism**.

Dr. Stephen Gilman for the translation from **Ideas sobre la novella**.

Finally, my gratitude to Marcelline Watson and Marilyn Croner for their editorial assistance.

# Contents

# INTRODUCTION

The elegant writing and important thinking of Nobel laureates, editors, writers, educators, publishers, and scientists come together here in common cause to affirm reading as humanity's most important tool, reading as vital to our survival and our growth.

The art of reading is put into a perspective for the human future, and science is called upon to explain how reading works in our minds and brains. New understandings of literature and education are presented.

The following articles reveal the second Gutenberg revolution, created by a new kind of people. These new people not only read from the vast numbers of books made possible by the first Gutenberg revolution, they also have the aesthetic abilities to create new internal dimensions of reality from reading.

If education is the process of being led out, then these new people are being led out to imaginatively fill up books rather than being filled up by information from books. Reading, just reading, can be an education for those inclined to develop their interior spaces.

What experiences await them? Perhaps a new world of people who will not require ideologies to defend their identities, who will transcend the walls of nationalism, racism and sexism and, perhaps, who won't feel the need to kill each other over their differences.

R. Patton Howell
Cross Timbers
Texas
June 1, 1990

### A Myriad Eyes

In reading great literature I become a thousand men and yet remain myself. Like a night sky in the Greek poem, I see with a myriad eyes, but it is still I who see. Here, as in worship, in love, in moral action, and in knowing, I transcend myself; and am never more myself than when I do.

—C. S. Lewis
*An Experiment in Criticism*

# The Environment of Reading

*No author ever spar'd a brother, Wits are gamecocks to one another.*

John Gay

*I know not, madam, that you have a right, upon moral principles, to make your readers suffer so much. (To Mrs. Sheridan)*

Samuel Johnson

*No publisher should ever express an opinion of the value of what he publishes. That is a matter entirely for the literary critic to decide.*

Oscar Wilde

*I could show you all society poisoned by this class of person—a class unknown to the ancients—who, not being able to find any honest occupation, be it manual labor or service, and unluckily knowing how to read and write, become the brokers of literature, live on our works, steal our manuscripts, falsify them, and sell them.*

Voltaire

*A word is not the same with one writer as with another. One tears it from his guts. The other pulls it out of his overcoat pocket.*

Charles Peguy

*An author who speaks about his own books is almost as bad as a mother who talks about her own children.*

Benjamin Disraeli

*Never read any book that is not a year old.*

R. W. Emerson

*After being turned down by numerous publishers, he decided to write for posterity.*

George Ade,
American humorist

*I object to publishers: the one service they have done me is to teach me to do without them. They combine commercial rascality with artistic touchiness and pettiness, without being either good businessmen or fine judges of literature. All that is necessary in the production of a book is an author and a bookseller, without an intermediate parasite.*

George Bernard Shaw

*People say that life is the thing, but I prefer reading.*

Logan Pearsall Smith

*I don't believe in publishers . . . like Methodists they love to keep the Sabbath and everything else they can lay their hands on.*

Amanda Ross

*Literary success of any enduring kind is made by refusing to do what publishers want, by refusing to write what the public wants, by refusing to accept any popular standard, by refusing to write anything to order.*

Lafcadio Hearn,
expatriate American writer

*'Tis the good reader that makes the good book.*

R. W. Emerson

*Just get it down on paper, and then we'll see what to do with it.*

Maxwell Perkins

*Great editors do not discover nor produce great authors; great authors create and produce great publishers.*

John Farrar

*An editor is one who separates the wheat from the chaff and prints the chaff.*

Adlai Stevenson

*I read part of it all the way through.*

attr. Samuel Goldwyn

# *1 Reading As Art*

# *Reading Books*

LEWIS LAPHAM

*Mr. Lapham is
the widely known editor of **Harper's Magazine**. He has
written numerous essays for publications as varied as
**The Saturday Evening Post, National Review, Life,
Forbes, The New York Times, Fortune, The Wall
Street Journal,** and **Vanity Fair.** His books include
**Fortune's Child, Money and Class in America** and
his current, **Imperial Masquerade.***

On first opening a book I listen for the sound of a
human voice. By this device I am absolved from reading much
of what is published in a given year. Most writers make use of
institutional codes (academic, literary, political, bureaucratic,
technical) in which they send messages already deteriorating
into the half-life of yesterday's news. Their transmissions
remain largely unintelligible, and unless I must decipher them
for professional reasons, I am content to let them pass by. I listen instead for a voice in which I can hear the music of the
human improvisation as performed through 5,000 years on the
stage of recorded time.

I cannot read without a pencil in my hand, and in books
that I have liked I discover marginalia ten and twenty years
out-of-date, many of the observations revised at intervals of
two or three years to accord with shifting angles of perception.
In an edition of Flaubert's *Sentimental Education* I find a scrib-
bled note in what I take to be my handwriting at the age of
nineteen, a note subsequently crossed out and contradicted by
the remark "foolishly romantic." Usually I read three or four
books at the same time, preferably by authors of different centuries. It sometimes happens that I find myself reading about
different periods in the history of the same landscape
(Herodotus and T.E. Lawrence on the deserts of Arabia, George
Orwell and Samuel Johnson on the seductions of London);
when this device is compounded by the superimposition of
marginalia reaching across twenty years and written while
traveling in cities as unlike each other as Chicago and Ran-
goon, I begin to understand the analogy between music and
what modern physicists have in mind when they try to
describe the continuum of space and time.

As a student, and later as an editor and occasional writer
of reviews, I felt obliged to finish every book I began to read.
This I no longer do. If within the first few pages I cannot hear
the author's voice, no matter if he promises to introduce me to
the court of Cyrus or the inner councils of the Democratic
Party, I abandon him at the first convenient opportunity. I do

this even with authors of great reputation, preferring to blame myself for whatever fault can be assigned. After some years I return to the author in question in the hope that I have learned enough to appreciate his greatness. When I was twenty, I couldn't read Aldous Huxley or G. K. Chesterton. By the time I was thirty I no longer could read Hermann Hesse or F. Scott Fitzgerald.

I don't count myself a literary critic, which relieves me of the necessity of making judgments or forming consistent opinions. I can contradict myself without apology or embarrassment, and within a period of months I can declare a former enthusiasm inoperative. I look for writers with whom I can imagine myself holding a conversation, who have seen enough of the world to remark on its wonders and vanities without thinking that it has done them a disservice. It is for this reason that I prefer the ancient writers, who have survived the winnowing of time and the misfortune of inept translation. It is an understanding of the character of man that I seek, and so I don't much care whether the author chooses Paris in the 1840s or present-day Washington for his mise-en-scene.

As a defense against the whims of literary fashion, I have adopted the strategy of waiting at least three years before reading any book that receives unanimous acclaim or purports to tell an inside story. The truth, on first hearing, usually strikes most people as outrageous, indecent, and wrong, and so when I come across a book about which nobody can find anything unpleasant to say, I assume that it contains a comfortable sermon. I doubt the reliability of all inside stories, and the interval of three years allows sufficient time for the politician to lose an election or for the revelation of the moment to exhaust the engines of publicity.

The delay also grants sufficient time to modify my own ignorance. Among the ancient authors, the fogs of superstition take the form of religious or magical beliefs, through which, living at a later period in the history of science, I can sometimes see. The moderns entertain equivalent superstitions, but these take the form of social and political prejudices to which I am also subject. With a few contemporary writers (most notably Evan S. Connell Jr., Gordon Craig, Gabriel Garcia Marquez, Jorge Amado, Paul Johnson, Daniel Boorstin, Lewis Thomas, Heinz Pagels, Robert Stone), I know myself to be in the company of men wiser and less easily deceived than I; but in much of what falls under the rubric of modern literature, I hear little more than the quarreling of the faculty in a university English department.

Perhaps this is the fault of the age. The wonders of science tend to intimidate writers who feel they cannot locate a plausible image of man in what they see as the rubble of his history. Thus their despair, their choice of narrow argument, their retreat behind the walls of dogma, or into the warm and airless rooms of sexual fantasy. The ancient authors, at least those among them who remain in print, seem less frightened of the world. They approach the study of man as if he were a universe unto himself, so vast and so mysterious as to defy the promulgation of doctrine and the making of smaller mystifications to conceal the fear of an empty stage.

Having learned to admire the spaciousness of Montaigne, I have come to think that the most astonishing books are those that I can open at random. Books that must always be read in sequence I think of as mediocre, the tricks of a magician at a child's birthday party as compared with the musical navigations of the blue whale. No matter where I take up the essays of Montaigne, whether in the midst of a discussion of cannibals or of presumption, I do not feel that I have missed the first act. I notice the same effect with novels that I read more than once; I do not need to go back to the beginning to remember the baldness of Vautrin, the silence of Queequeg, or the ardent expectations of Dorothea Brooke.

From an author I admire I will listen to anything and everything, to reports of marvels at Tarentum, to accounts of emperors gone sick with cruelty, to stories of giant ants standing watch over treasures of Aztec gold, to explanations of the

revolution of 1848, to polemics against the music criticism of
Rameau's nephew. It is all the same story, all proof of the same
mind, which, if I am to believe the evidence of the evolutionary
records, is also my own. Cicero seems no less real to me than
Ronald Reagan. They inhabit the same continuum in which
everything takes place in the same instant and in which they
depend for their reality on an act of my imagination.

Despite yesterday's announcement from Washington, I
suspect that Cicero has more to do with the shaping of my politics that Ronald Reagan or *The New York Times*. As a boy I read
his philippics against Antony and Catiline; I will continue to
read his letters to Atticus long after Reagan has returned to California, revising my impression of politics in the light of later
commentaries, not on Reagan but on Caesar and the Gallic wars.

This is not merely a literary conceit. Cicero's execution
coincided with the failure of the Roman republic, which in turn
gave rise to the empire and its eventual ruin, which in turn
gave way to the barbarians and then to the Jesuits, who pro-
voked the mockery of Voltaire and the eighteenth-century
philosophers from whom Jefferson derived the ideas that
informed the writing of the Declaration of Independence.

If I knew enough about the art of history, I could begin
anywhere, working the thread backward and forward through
the loom of time, weaving the design of a single and continuous
narrative, always and everywhere present. If I possessed the
imagination of a poet or the knowledge of a biologist, perhaps I
could discern aspects of the design not only in every civilization
that man has had the temerity to raise up from the mud but also
within the life and metamorphosis of every individual.

I am told that in the space of nine months the human
embryo ascends through a sequence that replicates 50 million
years of evolution, that within the first six years of life the
human mind recapitulates the dream of its travels through the
5,000 years of the historical journey from Sumer. Occasionally I
am reminded of these distances when I glance into the eyes of a
child, or when I notice an expression on the face of an unknown

man or woman seen in a foreign town. I don't know why the pang of recognition strikes me more poignantly while traveling in another country. At home, among friends and familiar disso- nance, the human voice has a way of becoming muffled behind the screens of social convention. But in the pages of a book it always can declare itself in a tone as unmistakable as that of woodwinds of the sea.

Browsing among the shelves of a library, I can imagine myself surrounded by the sounds of an orchestra tuning its instruments. It is as if I were presented with the possibility of a thousand melodic lines, each of them subject to as many varia- tions, all of them forming a counterpoint with a thousand other melodic lines and variations that combine in a music of brave and tragic beauty.

# Reading Literature

JOSEPH BRODSKY

*Joseph Brodsky,*
*internationally famous poet, received the Nobel Prize*
*for Literature in 1987. He won the John D. and*
*Catherine T. MacArthur Foundation's award for his*
*works of "genius" in 1981. His prose works are also*
*recognized; in 1986 his book* **Less Than One**
*received the National Critics Book Award for criticism.*
*In 1972 Dr. Brodsky became an involuntary exile*
*from his native country, Russia, and since has*
*chiefly lived in the United States.*

If art teaches anything (to the artist, in the first place). it is the privateness of the human condition. Being the most ancient as well as the most literal form of private enterprise, it fosters in a man, knowingly or unwittingly, a sense of his uniqueness, of individuality, of separateness—thus turning him from a social animal into an autonomous "I." Lots of things can be shared: a bed, a piece of bread, convictions, a mistress, but not a poem by, say, Rainer Maria Rilke. A work of art, of literature especially, and a poem in particular, addresses man tete-a-tete, entering with him into direct free of any go-betweens-relations.

It is for this reason that art in general, literature especially, and poetry in particular, is not exactly favored by the champions of the common good, masters of the masses, heralds of historical necessity. For there, where art has stepped, where a poem has been read, they discover, in place of the anticipated consent and unanimity, indifference and polyphony; in place of the resolve to act, inattention and fastidiousness. In other words, into the little zeros with which the champions of the common good and the rules of the masses tend to operate, art introduces a "period, comma, and a minus," transforming each zero into a tiny human, albeit not always a pretty face.

The great Baratynsky, speaking of his Muse, characterized her as possessing an "uncommon visage." It's in acquiring this "uncommon visage" that the meaning of human existence seems to lie, since for this uncommonness we are, as it were, prepared genetically. Regardless of whether one is a writer or a reader, one's task consists first of all in mastering a life that is one's own, not imposed or prescribed from without, no matter how noble its appearance may be. For each of us is issued but one life, and we know full well how it all ends. It would be regrettable to squander this one chance on someone else's appearance, someone else's experience, on a tautology—regrettable all the more because the heralds of historical necessity, at whose urging a man may be prepared to agree to this tautology, will not go to the grave with him or give him so much as a thank you.

Language and, presumably, literature are things that are more ancient and inevitable, more durable than any form of social organization. The revulsion, irony, or indifference often expressed by literature towards the state is essentially a reaction of the permanent—better yet, the infinite—against the temporary, against the finite. To say the least, as long as the state permits itself to interfere with the affairs of literature, literature has the right to interfere with the affairs of the state. A political system, a form of social organization, as any system in general, is by definition a form of the past tense that aspires to impose itself upon the present (and often on the future as well); and a man whose profession is language is the last one who can afford to forget this. The real danger for a writer is not so much the possibility (and often the certainty) of persecution on the part of the state, as it is the possibility of finding oneself mesmerized by the state's features, which whether monstrous or undergoing changes for the better, are always temporary.

The philosophy of the state, its ethics—not to mention its aesthetics—are always "yesterday." Language and literature are always "today," and often particularly in the case where a political system is orthodox—they may even constitute "tomorrow." One of literature's merits is precisely that it helps a person to make the time of his existence more specific, to distinguish himself from the crowd of his predecessors as well as his like numbers, to avoid tautology—that is, the fate otherwise known by the honorific term, "victim of history." What makes art in general, and literature in particular, remarkable, what distinguishes them from life, is precisely that they abhor repetition. In everyday life you can tell the same joke trice and, thrice getting a laugh, become the life of the party. In art, though, this sort of conduct is called "cliche."

Art is a recoilless weapon, and its development is determined not by the individuality of the artist, but by the dynamics and the logic of the material itself, by the previous fate of the means that each time demand (or suggest) a qualitatively new aesthetic solution. Possessing its own genealogy, dynamics, logic, and future, art is not synonymous with, but at best parallel to history; and the manner by which it exists is by continually creating a new aesthetic reality. That is why it is often found "ahead of progress," ahead of history, whose main instrument is—should we not, once more improve upon Marx—precisely the cliche.

Nowadays, there exists a rather widely held view, postulating that in his work a writer, in particular a poet, should make use of the language of the street, the language of the crowd. For all its democratic appearance, and its palpable advantages for a writer, this assertion is quite absurd and represents an attempt to subordinate art, in this case, literature, to history. It is only if we have resolved that it is time for Homo Sapiens to come to a halt in his development that literature should speak the language of the people. Otherwise, it is the people who should speak the language of literature.

On the whole, every new aesthetic reality makes man's ethical reality more precise. For aesthetics is the mother of ethics; the categories of "good" and "bad" are, first and foremost, aesthetic ones, at least etymologically preceding the categories of "good" and "evil." If in ethics not "all is permitted," it is precisely because not "all is permitted" in aesthetics, because the number of colors in the spectrum is limited. The tender babe who cries and rejects the stranger or who, on the contrary, reaches out to him, does so instinctively, making an aesthetic choice, not a moral one.

Aesthetic choice is a highly individual matter, and aesthetic experience is always a private one. Every new aesthetic reality makes one's experience even more private; and this kind of privacy, assuming at times the guise of literary (or some other) taste, can in itself turn out to be, if not a guarantee, then a form of defense against enslavement. For a man with taste, particularly literary taste, is less susceptible to the refrains and the rhythmical incantations peculiar to any version of political demagogy. The point is not so much that virtue does not constitute a guarantee for producing a masterpiece, as that evil, especially political evil, is always a bad stylist. The more substantial an individual's aesthetic experience is, the sounder his taste, the sharper his moral focus, the freer—though not necessarily the happier—he is.

It is precisely in this applied, rather than Platonic sense, that we should understand Dostoevsky's remark that beauty will save the world, or Matthew Arnold's belief that we shall be saved by poetry. It is probably too late for the world, but for the individual man, there always remains a chance. An aesthetic instinct develops in man rather rapidly, for, even without fully realizing who he is and what he actually requires, a person instinctively knows what he doesn't like and what doesn't suit him. In an anthropological respect let me reiterate, a human being is an aesthetic creature before he is an ethical one. Therefore, it is not that art, particularly literature, is a by-product of our species' development, but just the reverse. If what distinguishes us from other members of the animal kingdom is speech, then literature—and poetry in particular, being the highest form of locution—is, to put it bluntly, the goal of our species.

I am far from suggesting the idea of compulsory training in verse composition; nevertheless, the subdivision of society into intelligentsia and "all the rest" seems to me unacceptable. In moral terms, this situation is comparable to the subdivision of society into the poor and the rich; but if it is still possible to find some purely physical or material grounds for the existence of social inequality, for intellectual inequality these are inconceivable. Equality in this respect, unlike in anything else, has been guaranteed to us by nature. I am speaking not of education, but of the education in speech, the slightest imprecision in which may trigger the intrusion of false choice into one's life. The existence of literature prefigures existence on literature's plane of regard—and not only in the moral sense, but lexically as well. If a piece of music still allows a person the possibility of choosing between the passive role of listener and the active one of performer, a work of literature—of the art which is, to use Montale's phrase, hopelessly semantic—dooms him to the role of performer only.

In this role, it would seem to me, a person should appear more often than in any other. Moreover, it seems to me that, as a result of the population explosion and the attendant, ever-increasing atomization of society (i.e., the ever-increasing isolation of the individual), this role becomes more and more inevitable for a person. I don't suppose that I know more about life than anyone of my age, but it seems to me that, in the capacity of an interlocutor, a book is more reliable than a friend or a beloved. A novel or a poem is not a monologue, but the conversation of a writer with a reader, a conversation I repeat, that is more private, excluding all others—if you will, mutually misanthropic. And in the moment of this conversation a writer is equal to a reader, as well as the other way around, regardless of whether the writer is a great one or not. This equality is the equality of consciousness. It remains with a person for the rest of his life in the form of memory, foggy or distinct, and, sooner or later, appropriately or not, it conditions a person's conduct. It's precisely this that I have in mind in speaking of the role of the performer, all the more natural for one because a novel or a poem is the product of mutual loneliness—of a writer or a reader.

In the history of our species, in the history of Homo Sapiens, the book is anthropological development, similar essentially to the invention of the wheel. Having emerged in order to give us some idea not so much of our origins as of what that sapiens is capable of, a book constitutes a means of transportation through the space of experience, at the sped of a turning page. This movement, like every movement, becomes a flight from the common denominator, from an attempt to elevate this denominator's line, previously never reaching higher than the groin, to our heart, to our consciousness, to our imagination. This flight is the flight in the direction of "uncommon visage," in the direction of the numerator, in the direction of autonomy, in the direction of privacy. Regardless of whose image we are created in, there are already five billion of us, and for a human being there is no other future save that outlined by art. Otherwise, what lies ahead is the past—the political one, first of all, with all its mass police entertainments.

In any event, the condition of society in which art in general, and literature in particular, are the property or prerogative of a minority appears to me unhealthy and dangerous. I am not appealing for the replacement of the state with the library, although this thought has visited me frequently; but there is no doubt in my mind that, had we been choosing our leaders on the basis of their reading experience and not their political programs, there would be much less grief on earth. It seems to me that a potential master of our fates should be asked, first of all, not about how he imagines the course of his foreign policy, but about his attitude toward Stendhal, Dickens, Dostoevsky. If only because the lock and stock of literature is indeed human diversity and perversity, it turns out to be a reliable antidote for any attempt—whether familiar or yet to be invented—toward a total mass solution to the problems of human existence. As a form of moral insurance, at least, literature is much more dependable than a system of beliefs or a philosophical doctrine.

Since there are not laws that can protect us from ourselves, no criminal code is capable of preventing a true crime against literature; though we can condemn the material suppression of literature—the persecution of writers, acts of censorship, the burning of books—we are powerless when it comes to its worst violation: that of not reading the books. For that crime, a person pays with his whole life; if the offender is a nation, it pays with its history. Living in the country I live in, I would be the first prepared to believe that there is a set dependency between a person's material well-being and his literary ignorance. What keeps me from doing so is the history of that country in which I was born and grew up. For, reduced to a cause-and-effect minimum, to a crude formula, the Russian tragedy is precisely the tragedy of a society in which literature turned out to be the prerogative of the minority; of the celebrated Russian intelligentsia.

I have no wish to enlarge upon the subject, no wish to darken this evening with thoughts of the tens of millions of human lives destroyed by other millions, since what occurred in Russia in the first half of the twentieth century occurred before the introduction of automatic weapons—in the name of the triumph of a political doctrine whose unsoundness is already manifested in the fact that it requires human sacrifice for its realization. I'll just say that I believe—not empirically, alas, but only theoretically—that, for someone who has read a lot of Dickens, to shoot his like in the name of some idea is more problematic than for someone who has read no Dickens and I am speaking precisely about reading Dickens, Sterne, Stendhal, Dostoevsky, Flaubert, Balzac, Melville, Proust, Musil, and so forth; that is, about literature, not literacy or education.

# The Poet and the Computer

NORMAN COUSINS

*Norman Cousins is
widely known for his extraordinary editorship of
The Saturday Review and for his many books,
among which were his best-selling book, The Anatomy
of an Illness, and The Human Adventure. His
latest book, also a bestseller is Head First: Biology
of Hope. For his wide-ranging efforts to foster the
good of the world community he was awarded the
United Nations Peace Medal.*

28

"A poet," said Aristotle, "has the advantage of expressing the universal; the specialist expresses only the particular." The poet, moreover, can remind us that man's greatest energy comes not from his dynamos but from his dreams. The notion of where a man ought to be instead of where he is; the liberation from cramped prospects; the intimations of immortality through art, all these proceed naturally out of dreams. But the quality of man's dreams can only be a reflection of his subconscious. What he puts into his subconscious, therefore, is quite literally the most important nourishment in the world.

Nothing really happens to a man except as it is registered in the subconscious. This is where event and feeling become memory and where the proof of life is stored. The poet, and I use the term to include all those who have respect for and speak to the human spirit, can help to supply the subconscious with material to enhance its sensitivity, thus safeguarding it. The poet, too, can help to keep man from making himself over in the image of his electronic marvels. The danger is not so much that man will be controlled by the computer as that he may imitate it.

There once was a time, in the history of this society, when the ability of people to convey meaning was enriched by their knowledge of and access to the work of creative minds from across the centuries. No more. Conversation and letters today, like education, have become enfeebled by emphasis on the functional and the purely contemporary. The result is a mechanization not just of the way we live but of the way we think and of the human spirit itself.

The delegates to the United States Constitutional Convention were able to undergird their arguments with allusions to historical situations and to the ideas of philosophers, essayists, and dramatists. Names such as Thucydides, Aristotle, Herodotus, Plutarch, or Seneca were commonly cited to support their positions. They alluded to fictional characters from Aristophanes, Marlowe, or Shakespeare to lend color to the exploration of ideas. The analytical essays by Hamilton, Madison, and Jay that appeared in *The Federalist Papers* were an excursion into the remote corners of history.

Men such as Jefferson, Adams, Franklin, and Rush, could summon pertinent quotations from Suetonius or Machiavelli or Montaigne to illustrate a principle. If they referred to Bacon's opinion of Aristotle, they didn't have to cite particulars; they assumed such details were common knowledge. Their allusions were not the product of intellectual ostentation or ornamentation but the natural condiments of discourse, bringing out the full flavor of the cultivated intelligence.

The same was true of correspondence. People regarded letters as an art form and a highly satisfying way of engaging in civilized exchange. The correspondence of Jefferson and Adams and Priestley was not so much a display of personal matters as a review of the human condition. It was not unusual for the writers to range across the entire arena of human thought as a way of sharing perceptions. Allusion was common currency. Today, we rarely turn to letters as a way of embarking on voyages of intellectual discovery.

The essential problem of man in a computerized age remains the same as it has always been. That problem is not solely how to be more productive, more comfortable, more content, but how to be more sensitive, more sensible, more proportionate, more alive. The computer makes possible a phenomenal leap in human proficiency; it demolishes the fences around the practical and even the theoretical intelligence. But the question persists, and indeed grows, whether the computer makes it easier or harder for human beings to know who they really are, to identify their real problems, to respond more fully to beauty, to place adequate value on life, and to make their world safer than it now is.

Electronic brains can reduce the profusion of dead ends involved in vital research. But they can't eliminate the foolishness and decay that come from the unexamined life. Nor do they connect a man to the things he has to be connected to, the reality of pain in others; the possibilities of creative growth in himself; the memory of the race; and the rights of the next generation.

The reason these matters are important in a computerized age is that there may be a tendency to mistake data for wisdom, just as there has always been a tendency to confuse logic with values and intelligence with insight. Unobstructed access to facts can produce unlimited good only if it is matched by the desire and ability to find out what they mean and where they would lead.

Facts are terrible things if left sprawling and unattended. They are too easily regarded as evaluated certainties rather than as the rawest of raw materials crying to be processed into the texture of logic. It requires a very unusual mind, Whitehead said, to undertake the analysis of a fact. The computer can provide a correct number, but it may be an irrelevant number until judgment is pronounced.

To the extent, then, that man fails to make the distinction between the intermediate operations of electronic intelligence and the ultimate responsibilities of human decision and conscience, the computer could obscure man's awareness of the need to come to terms with himself. It may foster the illusion that he is asking fundamental questions when actually he is asking only functional ones. It may be regarded as a substitute for intelligence instead of an extension of it. It may promote undue confidence in concrete answers. "If we begin with certainties," Bacon said, "we shall end in doubts; but if we begin with doubts, and we are patient with them, we shall end in certainties."

The computer knows how to vanquish error, but before we lose ourselves in celebration of victory, we might reflect on the great advances in the human situation that have come about because men were challenged by error and would not stop thinking and probing until they found better approaches for dealing with it. "Give me a good fruitful error, full of seeds, bursting with its own corrections," Ferris Greenslet wrote. "You can keep your sterile truth for yourself."

Without taking anything away from the technicians, it might be fruitful to effect some sort of junction between the computer technologist and the poet. A genuine purpose may be served by turning loose the wonders of the creative imagination on the kinds of problems being put to electronic tubes and transistors. The company of poets may enable the men who tend the machines to see a larger panorama of possibilities than technology alone may inspire.

Poets remind men of their uniqueness. It is not necessary to possess the ultimate definition of this uniqueness. Even to speculate on it is a gain.

# 2 Reading And Reader

# The Evolution of the Novel

NATHAN MITCHELL

*Dr. Mitchell*
*has been a theologian, monk, professor of English*
*at Notre Dame and the managing editor*
*of Saybrook Publishers. Besides his many scholarly*
*articles, his published books include* **Rite of Penance**
*and* **Mission and Ministry***.*

There are, of course, ways in which all narrative, all story, involves the creation of mental reality by readers. Here, we suggest the "novel" as a supreme example of this thrust, and more, as a kind of narrative that was not possible at an earlier period in the evolutionary development of mind in the human species.

Already in classical literatures (Greek epics, Hebrew sagas of the patriarchs), novelistic elements are at work: plot and subplot, character development, conflicts and resolution, psychological drama, the portrayal of feelings arising from within characters who have become quite real to the reader/listener. One thinks of I-II Samuel, for example, which is essentially a novel about King David and the Jerusalem court written in two books.

However, these earlier literatures usually require a referent (or set of referents) from outside the story itself in order to legitimate the story's action, characters and significance. This referent may be either implied or explicit, but it is always there, powerfully guiding the reader's response to the story and providing the correct interpretation of the novel's plots and characters. In the case of I-II Samuel, this external referent is primarily a theological one. The reader is invited (indeed, commanded) to understand the narrative events as displays of special care for Israel by the God of Abraham, Isaac and Jacob who now chooses David as his elect, anointed one (and David's heirs as the legitimate holders of royal power in the land). In short, this is a novel with a very specific theological agenda and the reader is required to approach the book with at least the willingness to accept the story as valid, true, fraught with implications for his/her present existence. The external referent guides, limits and bends the reader's response. Indeed, it binds the readers to the story, marking out for them what is "real" from what is illusory. It beckons readers to live within that "real" world and suggests the consequences of a refusal to do so.

A similar phenomenon is present in those "epic poetry novels" of classical Greece and Rome, the *Odyssey* and the *Aeneid*. In these, the external referent may better be called a political one. These are novels which narrate and interpret the political origins and genius of a people, the source of their national cohesion, and the reasons for their power in the world. They have a strong "identity-creating" junction. And somewhat like the Hebrew novels, they bind readers to the story by suggesting (indeed, insisting) that the conditions for "real" life in the world are met, for the Greek or the Roman, only through identification with the proto-myths and proto-heroes of the story. These early Hebrew and Greek/Roman novels are not, then, strictly self-contained worlds. They have an opening at the end that ties them intimately to the political/theological concerns and fortunes of the people who created them. Indeed, the story has a loop which binds in the present actions and attitudes of the readers. On such conditions, the loss of the story would imply a loss of identity, loss of self. The self (both individual and collective) is bound to the story.

Archaic novels of this type suggest a particular understanding of the act of reading. To read I-II Samuel or the *Odyssey* is an act of anamnesis. The reader is pulled toward memory, bound to memory by the ever-present (if only implied) external referent. The act of reading becomes an act of anamnetic repetition. This understanding of what reading is is further reinforced when one recalls that the contexts which gave rise to this literature, as well as the environment within which it was read, were strongly cultic/ritual/public. These proto-novels were hieratic, sacred works, looped around both the "itself" and the readers in a closed circle of memory. The reader was an inevitable participant in the story itself, and without his participation the circle could not close, the self could not be identified, and life in any "real" sense could not continue. Quite literally, reading in this archaic sense was a life-and-death matter. (One is reminded that the anthropologist Richard Leakey argued in his book *Origins* that the thing which permitted the first tentative tribes of Homo Sapiens to survive was the ability to carry with themselves four essential elements: food, fire, water, and experience embedded in (bound to) language.

The novel in the modern sense does not, however, require an external referent in order to validate its world, nor does it require a closed circle of memory in order to legitimate or guarantee the reader's response. The modern novel's inventions, its world of characters, plots, physical and mental furnishings are self-validating, self-legitimating. Readers are not bound to the modern novel as they are bound to the stories of its archaic predecessors. The closed loop of memory gives way to an open field, a space within which readers can construct their own mental reality out of the novel's raw stuff. There is no sanctioned interpretation compelled by an external referent which exists outside the novel and independently of it. The modern novel is thus, if you will, hermeneutically emancipated and resists all privileged interpretations. (This may sadden critics, but will surely delight robust readers.) Or put another way, the modern novel is hermeneutically pluralistic and can accommodate a virtually limitless range of reader responses, none of which need to be subjected to censorship. The adequacy of a reader's response may be open to evaluation, since its quality depends on a reader's skill. This hermeneutically open character of the modern novel means there is no sanctioned key for readers to find (no legitimating external referent that unlocks meaning and experience from the text). Both the author and the reader of the modern novel are self-inventors: indeed, they may be said to co-invent the work. Nor can the author claim to empower the reader's invention, for that inventiveness comes from the reader's own innate capacity to fabulate a mental world, to furnish and people it from the author's clues.

The reason for this shift from archaic to modern in the novel is, I suspect, rooted in a more fundamental shift in the evolutionary development of mind in the human species and, concomitantly, with a shift in the understanding of the self. Self-consciousness (self-awareness, self-reflective awareness) is generally assumed to distinguish our species from our animal ancestors in the natural world. The achievement of such self-consciousness simultaneously empowered humans to behave in ways unparalleled among the animals and betrayed our origins in isolating us from the rest of this planet's inhabitants. Humans now possessed a mind quite unbound from its immediate environment, capable of stepping back from that environment to examine its own existence and activities. Now, humans had not only fear but awareness of fear; they not only died, they were aware of death as the inescapable horizon against which all else in life takes place.

It is well known, too, that the achievement (which is also a betrayal of origins) of human self-consciousness was not a singularly meteoric ascent. It has been an evolution, still presumably ongoing, punctuated by both forward motion and slippage, conquest and compromise. The achieved self of the human being remains a fragile construction, ever capable of collapsing and being crushed under its own pilasters. The bad news about self-consciousness is that it is never secure, never finished, and cannot, in any world we know, survive. Small wonder, then, that the human species learned rather early on to crush the grape, ferment its juice and imbibe oblivion.

Further, the emergence of self-consciousness set our species a task with which our animal ancestors did not need to amuse themselves: the task of establishing individual selfhood, identity, personality. One of the charms of animals is their total absorption with being simply what they are. Their time is utterly and completely spent in catness, dogness and the like. Ours is not, alas; strangely our unbound mental capacities chain us to the tasks of self-invention. We must learn the art of the deal, create a persona for the media, seek meaningful relationships, mourn their absence or loss, fight city hall and write books.

The art of modern writing is, indeed, a premier means of carrying on the task of self-invention. The modern art of reading lets us create words of living people within our minds. This evolution makes possible the limitless expansion of the self and has transformed the significance of reading.

# Sacred Books

## WEBSTER KITCHELL HOWELL

*Dr. Howell is
the minister of The First Unitarian Church of Lancaster,
Pennsylvania. He is the author of scholarly articles
and is editor of Consciousness, The Universe Within,
to be published in 1991.*

People have always experienced moments of intense meaning in life, wherein one is drawn outside of one's self to a point of transcendent perspective so that things like purpose and meaning in life become self-evident.

Given this ancient and ongoing experience, we can see that somebody simultaneously invented religion and story-telling. Because, though an initial experience of intense meaning in life might be classified as pure grace, it was through a story that this meaning could be called forth not only from the storyteller but from the listeners. Whereas before storytelling the experience of being transported outside one's self was purely a question of fate or happenstance or grace, now a story could facilitate this essential journey out of the self to a place where perspective and, thus meaning of life, could be pursued. Ultimately, books reflect this journey and in doing so, they engender it.

As a matter of fact, all religion and all literature stem from a core story of some kind and our cultural heritage is no different. The Judeo-Christian story is very much based on the journey outside of the self to find that the quality of reality is not chaotic or oppressive but is connected. The essential story is a journey from self where one is imprisoned by a lack of perspective, to where the self is enabled to participate in life rather than be chased and chained by the ghost of one's own possibilities.

As a matter of fact, this is why the Jews are chosen in the *Old Testament*. They have a story, that incredibly magic thing. Through it, they have a God of their fathers' and the story itself as the mechanism which can lead them to what that God is all about. It leads them to life. In truth, the Jews are named by a story as are we all in one way or another. We all have our own stories and, in addition, most everyone has his or her own bible, his or her own written version of a story, a mechanism which has somehow been essential to one's own particular journey outside of oneself. They each have their special book.

I suppose the first special book for me was the *Child's Biography of James Fenimore Cooper*. A strange thing began to happen to me as I read this book. I began to really read. Up to this point in the fourth grade, I could read, but only a word at a time. I could take a word up off a page and feed it into my brain. But this book was magic, because there I was plodding away, and then, before I knew it, I was closing the book and it was dinner time. I had been away on a trip. I had been living at Jim's house and playing with him, and it was as if I hadn't read the book at all, but rather some magic part of me had, my imagination. My imagination didn't read words, but rather sentences, paragraphs, pages, stories. Every noun against a verb was a story which built bigger stories and only the imagination could grasp and leap into that other world and explore its limits. It was almost as if the book outlined a country on a map. It was a structure, a mechanism which triggered my imagination, and my imagination, pulling a lifetime of experience behind it, went into that outline on the map and filled it in. That filling in was a journey beyond the self.

There is only one qualifier to this process. A book or a story is only as good or transforming as we are willing to dwell within it. A story can affect us only if we are willing to crawl inside it and fill it in with our own imagination and experience.

Whenever I see a science fiction movie or a TV show which shows future people discussing books, the books are usually presented as archaic systems containing information. Books do contain information, some of which we retain. But the purpose of books and stories is not, and never has been, to be storage containers. For example, the Bible was never meant to be the ancient version of a video tape. It is compiled of stories. It is a story. Its purpose is not to fill us up but rather the opposite. We fill it up. And the books which mean the most to us are the ones we put the most of ourselves into. Any book or story, including the Bible, which can enable that process is divine. It is life saving, for we are drawn out of ourselves. This applies to escapist books, dirty books, philosophy books, comic books, it even applies to text books.

However, it's here we have to stop and get critical. There are some bad books out there. A book can seem bad for two reasons: One, there is something really wrong with it so that it actually short-circuits the journey outside the self. Or two, there is something wrong with the way we are relating to the book. In relation to this second point about how we relate to a book, it's important to remember that it's because of the leap of our imagination that books and stories are transforming, not the other way around. Books are vessels to be filled by us. It's when we forget this that our Bibles sometimes fail us, and we blame the book. We often feel as though a book is somehow complete into itself, and we feel let down when we find out it isn't. There is a sense of betrayal that goes along with this. People are betrayed by something they put a lot of themselves into, which they trusted to be true in some absolute way, and it just didn't work out. Most of us have love affairs with books which have come to "let us down." For example, when I was in the sixth grade, J. D. Salinger's *A Catcher in the Rye* was, for me, the most infallible piece of literature that could be written. Holden Caulfield was an adolescent's dream. Through Holden Caulfield I could tell people, especially adults, what they could go do with themselves and where they gave me a royal pain. But by the eighth grade, I thought the whole thing was pretentious. Holden Caulfield was really kind of immature and J. D. Salinger had really just snowed me with all the "jive" talk. Though I have rediscovered J. D. Salinger over and over again, at that time, I became a little ashamed of myself for being so un-independent to think that Holden Caulfield could be the depth and breadth of existence.

This same kind of thing often happens when people discover that the Bible isn't literally true. Indeed this is always what happens when we rely on a book or a story to be authoritative and complete unto itself. It lets us down. It doesn't take us on the journey outside of ourselves, because we expect it to have done all the work and made all the discoveries for us. When we relate to books in this way we remain in ourselves. We betray ourselves.

That covers the second critical point about a bad book, when it's our fault. But what about the first critical point, about a book that is just bad? A bad book is one which helps us stay inside ourselves. These are the self-books, the Body books, and all the "pop" psychology books. They all tell you how you can be fulfilled, how you can be healthy, how you can be happy. In their own way, they all posit cures for fear and existential nausea. One doesn't go beyond the self, one just fixes it up, tones it up, makes it okay, gives it a hug today. Instead of being transcended, the self is deodorized. These are by far the best-selling books in America today. The self-books outsell every other kind of book on the market. These books take you on a journey to yourself, not the interconnected self, just the self. It's a short trip. These books are the closest thing to verbal video games that we have. Just as TV and video games stretch your imagination to an average of 24 inches, the *me* books stretch you to about as tall and wide as you presently are.

On the other hand, the books that last are either re-tellings of that primal story about the journey out of the self, or critiques of that primal story. This covers most myths, novels, poems, essays, scientific explications, philosophies and jokes put to paper. The reason these books last is not because they're good or art. They last because they work. They are channels of transformation. They get us outside of ourselves. For the most part, books are like soldiers on the front lines of consciousness in the war against meaninglessness in life. Books are more than a medium, like film. Rather, they are a primordial reflection of how we think. Unlike any other medium, books as a whole, in their utilization of symbols to tell stories, invite and facilitate the evolution of consciousness. They facilitate a life-saving way of thinking which points outward, creating a stance which is world inclusive rather than world exclusive. Books are sacred; they are sacraments. As Keats said, they are our phoenix wings to fly at our own desire.

# A Singular Experience

## PETER KOESTENBAUM

*Peter Koestenbaum is*
*the world-famous philosopher to business. His best-*
*selling **The Heart of Business** has been translated*
*internationally and is used by corporate giants*
*around the world. Donald Petersen, president of*
*Ford Motor Company, reflects: "People,*
*Dr. Koestenbaum says, need to feel worthy—*
*to have values, principles, integrity."*

How much does reading and understanding really help in coping with the world? Are reading and doing incompatible? Are they discernibly different? Could reading be a form of doing? Is it true that we must change ourselves before we can change others? That we must be different before the world can be different? Or is that rationalization, an anodyne for our impotence ... or even laziness?

Let us explore and experiment. Here we invoke what we might call an updated version of the philosophy of the German thinker from the early nineteenth century, Arthur Schopenhauer. But if you know him or other thinkers grounded on biology and evolution, you will find these thoughts a bit easier.

The mind of man and woman is a product of biological evolution, and that mind rebels against its ancestry. Consciousness has developed a sense of equity, of justice, and of fairness. The mind adheres to a constellation of values which is independent of the rules of biology, survival, evolution and cosmic indifference. Reading is the yearning towards meaning. It is what happens when the mind is in unresolved dissonance with reality. Reading is the response to the emergency which occurs when two products of evolution, mind and nature, clash and must find their resolving harmony.

In understanding that meaning, a few principles suffice. And they are really metaphors; they are symbols. They are poetic ways, if you will, of organizing the world into significance for us. But this life force is not unique or isolated. It is not limited to the biological order. It is not restricted to what we call life. Better yet, we are entitled to call life everything that exhibits energy, potential or kinetic. The life force derives from the geological order. And that derives from the orders of astronomy and cosmology, the science of all there is. The inert bodies of the universe manifest physical energy; the sun, the galaxies, the winds, the heat and the cold, the forces within the atom and the gravitational attraction among the planets, the moving plates under the earth, the hot magnum within, the rains of the sky and the tides of the ocean, the exploding supernovae and the imploding black holes. All these forces, part of one universal force, swirl, move, wave and weave with infinite power.

Life is but an outgrowth of that. We should call these movements, these changes, some ominous and other generous, not the life force but the universal energy. It feels like one thing, one event, one phenomenon, one state of affairs. We have a singular name for the universal energy because it appears to us as a unifying reality. It is the mind, the product, the crowning glory of that energy itself.

Reading that resolves mind and nature is to be the energy, to express the energy, to manifest it, and no more and no less. This is the meaning of reading. This energy is, wants to be, and must be. And the more it is what it is, the more it is also fulfilled.

We, human beings, participate in this energy. We are this energy. It is one, but that oneness moves nevertheless in all directions. As we identify with that energy, we also sense our unity with all of nature. And that perception gives us one of our senses of immortality, or better, of eternity. It is the knowledge that we have always been and always will be, although in what may appear—but appear only—to be different forms.

We are consciousness. And as such we are self-conscious. We are aware of being conscious. We are more than the world energy, we are also aware of the world energy. And just as the energy is wild, so is the consciousness of it peaceful. And just as the life force is hysterical, so is our consciousness of it tranquil. And our understanding of that consciousness has been developed through silent reading. It is the source of our sense of immortality, our feeling of eternity.

And the singular consciousness, which is you and I, is part of the universal consciousness, the world mind or the world reason. And that is an eternal concept, a concept of eternity. The universal mind—vast as it is, and it is infinitely vast—is nevertheless a singular experience. That is why in all the great visions of being, the world religions, we have had monotheism. And we, in our singularity, replicate that cosmic singularity. All the other singularities within the world, the other centers of life and of consciousness, are like mirrors within mirrors within mirrors, all of them reflecting the same image, the same truth. The one and the many are indistinguishable. During his religious and metaphysical moments, the great seventeenth century mathematician Leibnitz called these "monads," and his total view the "monadology." He meant that the solitary universal mind is accurately reflected in the plurality of every single individual mind. The world is like a million raindrops, each reflecting the very same landscape.

How do we know this? Through internalizing reading, its symbols and images. These images represent deep truths; they express insights we can confirm through sensitive introspection. They fit. They resolve. We say, "Aha!" And through them we find a final answer to the problem of existence.

Through reading we create extreme experiences, which open for us the eyes of the heart and divulge a more profound truth, confirm these solutions. These extreme experiences are anxiety, will, passion, ethics, and grace. When in their presence, we are willing to revise the science of the universe to accommodate not only facts, but our subjective interior realities. And that is how religion and philosophy are born, and that is how the arts are confirmed. Novalis said poetry is the true science, for these are the things that matter most.

# 3 Reading And Science

# The Literary World of Nonlocal Mind

LARRY DOSSEY

*Dr. Dossey is
a diplomate of the American Board of Internal Medicine
and is former president of the Isthmus Institute. He is
author of numerous articles and books including Space,
Time and Medicine, has received widespread attention
and has been translated into several languages. His current book, Reclaiming the Soul, calls for a radical new
theory of the human mind and a redefinition of human
mental function. Dr. Dossey travels widely as a public
speaker, in addition to pursuing his practice of internal
medicine. He lives in Dallas with his wife, Barbara, who
is the author of several award-winning books.*

... the psyche's attachment to the brain, i.e., its space-
time limitation, is no longer as self-evident and incontro-
vertible as we have hitherto been led to believe ... An
objective and critical survey of the available data would
establish that perceptions occur as if in part there were no
space, in part no time ... anyone who does justice to the
facts cannot but admit that their apparent space-timeless-
ness is their most essential quality ... It is not only
permissible to doubt the absolute validity of space-time
perception; it is, in view of the available facts, even
imperative to do so.

—C. G. Jung

The idea that the brain is the seat and source of the mind
goes almost unchallenged within science today. This influential
idea really is ancient and can be found, even, in the Hippocratic
writings. Today we "know" that our consciousness is depen-
dent on the brain's chemistry; disturb it and our thought processes and level of awareness can be changed, sometimes
wildly.

These observations buttress the assumption in our culture
that the mind is entirely "local"—i.e., it is confined or localized
to points in space (the brain and body) and time (the present
moment and the single lifetime). Put simply, the mind is in the
here-and-now. It cannot go wandering off; it stays home in the
brain and body and in the present.

These local beliefs about the mind, although they have
traditionally carried great weight, can no longer be taken for
granted. In fact, evidence suggests that the mind is not local,
either in space or in time. And as we shall see, this view has
vast implications.

This is not the place to review all the reasons which call
for a nonlocal view of the human mind, but I will briefly mention some pieces to the puzzle. First, there is the problem of

localizing the mind to the head. Let me give you an idea of how difficult this is. As everyone knows today, there is a class of chemicals called the endorphins, which are made in the brain and which contribute to our mental life. They affect our mood, what we call our "feelings" and even pain perception. Yet it has been recently discovered that there are receptors for these chemicals, as well as the capacity to manufacture them on sites distant from the brain—on various types of white blood cells and at points scattered throughout the G.I. tract from the esophagus to the anus. This means that there apparently is brain-like tissue scattered throughout the body suggesting the existence of two kinds of brains—the *anatomic* brain that sits inside the cranium, and the *functional* brain that includes the anatomic brain but distant tissue as well that possesses brain-like function.

Recall that these chemicals, the endorphins, affect our emotions and feelings, which make up part of what we generally mean by "mind." So what are we to say? The conclusion may be that we've had it wrong by confining "mind" solely to the brain. It appears to be beyond the brain and into the body—skin, hands, feet, legs, liver, spleen, you name it. We face the possibility that the entire body is alive with mind, since there are few tissues in the body that are bloodless.

The location of these mind-related chemicals in the gut has led Candace Pert, chief of brain chemistry at the National Institute of Mental Health, to ask whether this may be the reason we have always spoken of "gut feelings" or of "feeling it in the gut." But why only the gut? Perhaps we can also begin to consider that feelings could originate in any part of the body.

Where *do* we feel? And think? The question is now open. It cannot be considered improper to ask whether "messages" from any part of the body are not just metaphor but literal fact. Maybe Hesse was right when he claimed, in the prologue to *Demian*, to have learned to listen to the whisperings of his blood.

Among modern thinkers who considered a nonlocal view of mind was Gregory Bateson who observed: " The individual mind is immanent but not only in the body. It is immanent also in pathways and messages outside the body."

To the above views could be added an endless list of visionaries, poets, mystics, and seers of virtually every spiritual tradition we know about, which echoes the same theme: the mind is not confined to individuals; it is nonlocal in space and time; when we regard it only as a function of an isolated person, we are engaging in a grave error.

Not only does the mind appear to have broken the confines of the cranium and spread throughout the body, it seems to have leaped the boundaries of the body itself, as well as the restrictions of the present moment. For a decade, studies done at Princeton University's Engineering Anomalies Research Laboratory have shown that minds can communicate messages in stunning detail even when separated by up to 6,000 miles; and the "receiving" mind can "get" the information up to three days *before* it is sent. Moreover, spatial separation between persons has not proved fundamental in certain studies in clinical medicine. Praying persons who were widely separated from critically ill patients were able to exert strong statistical effects on their clinical courses in a sophisticated double-blind, prospective, controlled study.

Why is the nature of the mind important in thinking about the place of reading in a culture? Why does it really matter if human consciousness behaves locally or nonlocally? One of the main reasons is that we need some rational way to envision how "the information gets around" in cultures. How does the spread take place? By some kind of domino theory in which individual, isolated minds react one by one to some cultural event or process, and then interact with each other? Is information passed along from one person to another, like germs? I suspect this explanation is to clumsy to explain the impact of literature within cultures because it contains an erroneous assumption—that minds are local entities, confined to the brains and bodies of single persons, and that information can be gained only in ways explainable by sensory cues.

But what if the limitations of brains and bodies on the mind are not absolute? What if minds are fundamentally unbounded in space and time? What if physicist Erwin Schrodinger was correct in claiming,

Mind is by its very nature is a *singulartantum*. I should say: the overall number of minds is just one. . . . To divide or multiply consciousness is something meaningless. In all the world, there is no kind of framework within which we can find consciousness in the plural; this is simply something we construct because of the spatio-temporality of individuals, but it is a false construction . . .

Today the world is reeling from political, social, and cultural changes, particularly in eastern Europe, that were completely unanticipated by experts. Various ad hoc hypotheses are tirelessly being invented to "explain" these upheavals. For instance, it is now claimed in retrospect that there were economic forces we should have recognized all along, that would have allowed prediction. Various informational factors are suggested—FAX and copy machines, smuggled video tapes, books and magazines, satellite-beamed television programs, radio, the list is endless—that may have triggered the changes. These hypothesized factors have one thing in common: They are all "local." They assume that minds are confined to individual persons and that the spread of information is therefore entirely explainable on a sensory basis.

But this view is in conflict with much data pointing to nonlocal qualities of the human mind. Would a nonlocal view of consciousness help explain the ecology of these sweeping changes? Perhaps. Such a view would not be incompatible with the local view, for astonishing amounts of information obviously can be transmitted from person to person by purely sensory means. The advantages of a nonlocal view, however, are several. It would be consistent with emerging data suggesting that the mind can behave on occasion as if unbounded in space and time. It could predict that information could sometimes by "transmitted" instantly, leapfrogging the presumed barriers imposed by linear space and flowing time. It would predict that isolation of minds—and thus of information—is intrinsically impossible.

What about reading? Nonlocal theories of the mind would no longer regard it as a purely personal experience. It would be an entry node where information might enter into the unbounded, *One Mind* of which Schrodinger spoke. Reading would always contain the possibility, at least, of being a shared, collective experience—and a potentially explosive one at that—which the censors and bookburners of history have always seemed to understand.

When we understand the flow of information within cultures, it is unlikely to be explainable within the customary local frameworks now used to describe the mind. All around us is evidence that consciousness is unbounded in space and time, unrestricted to persons, not confined to the here-and-now. Any theory pretending to explain the impact of reading on culture that relies solely on a local model of mental function is going to be seriously limited, probably even wrong.

# *Mental Reality*

SIR JOHN ECCLES
AND ROGER SPERRY

*Sir John Eccles and Dr. Roger Sperry
are Nobel laureates. They came together, each having
one piece of a mosaic which combined might lay the
groundwork for a scientific understanding of mind as
reality. What follows is three segments of conversations
between these two authors at the Isthmus Institute.
Among Sir John's numerous books is **The Wonder
of Being Human.** Dr. Sperry's words may be
found in **The Reach of the Mind.***

## Dr. Sperry

The whole world of inner experience (the world of the humanities) long rejected by twentieth century scientific materialism becomes recognized and included within the domain of science. Basic revisions in concepts of causality are involved here; the whole, besides being "different from and greater than the sum of the parts," also causally determines the fate of the parts, without interfering with the physical or chemical laws for the subentities at their own level. It follows that physical science no longer perceives the world to be reducible to quantum mechanics or to any other unifying ultra element or field force. The qualitative, holistic properties at all different levels become causally real in their own form and have to be included in the causal account. Quantum theory on these terms no longer replaces or subsumes classical mechanics but rather just supplements or complements.

Conscious or mental phenomena are dynamic, emergent, pattern properties of the living brain in action—a point accepted by many, including some of the more tough-minded brain researchers. Second, my argument goes a critical step further, and insists that these emergent pattern properties in the brain have causal control potency—just as they do elsewhere in the universe. And there we have the answer to the age-old enigma of consciousness.

To put it very simply, it becomes a question largely of who pushes whom around in the population of causal forces that occupy the cranium. There exists within the human cranium a whole world of diverse causal forces; what is more, there are forces within forces within forces, as in no other cubic half-foot of universe that we know. At the lowermost levels in this system are those local aggregates of subnuclear particles confined with the neutrons and protons of their respective atomic nuclei. These individuals, of course, don't have very much to say about what goes on in the affairs of the brain. Like the atomic nucleus and its associated electrons, the subnuclear and other atomic elements are "molecule-bound" for the most part, and get hauled and pushed around by the larger spatial and configurational forces of the whole molecule.

Similarly the molecular elements in the brain are themselves pretty well bound up, moved and ordered about by the enveloping properties of the cells within which they are located. Along with their internal atomic and subnuclear parts, the brain molecules are obliged to submit to a course of activity in time and space that is determined very largely by the overall dynamic and spatial properties of the whole brain cell as an entity. Even the brain cells, however, with their long fibers and impulse conducting elements, do not have very much to say either about when or in what time pattern, for example, they are going to fire their messages. The firing orders come from a higher command.

The flow and the timing of impulse traffic through any cell, or nucleus of cells, in the brain is governed very largely by the overall encompassing properties of the whole cerebral circuit system, and also by the relationship of this system to other circuit systems. Even the circuit properties of the cerebral system as a whole, and the way in which these govern the flow pattern of impulse traffic throughout—that is, the circuit properties of the whole brain—may undergo radical and widespread changes with just the flick of a cerebral facilitatory "set." This set is a shifting pattern of central excitation that will open or prime one group of circuit pathways while at the same time closing, repressing, or inhibiting endless other circuit potentialities. Such changes of set are involved in a "shift of attention," "a turn of thought," "a change of feeling," or "a new insight," etc. In short, if one climbs upward through the chain of command within the brain, one finds at the very top those overall organizational forces and dynamic properties of the large patterns of cerebral excitation that constitute the mental or psychic phenomena.

### Sir John Eccles

Let me approach Dr. Sperry's subject from a different angle. We have the indubitable experience that by thinking and willing we can control our actions if we so wish, such actions being called voluntary movements. The sequence can be expressed as motive (thinking), intention (willing), voluntary action. In bringing about movement voluntarily some brain events are initiated. There is the well-known crossed pyramidal tract from the motor cortex down the spinal cord to the nerve cells of the opposite side that cause the muscles to contract. The motor cortex is a narrow band of the cerebral cortex running over its convexity from the midline near the vertex. The left motor cortex controls the right side of the body and vice versa.

It might be thought that voluntary movement is so explained, but the reality is enormously more complicated and only partly understood. The pyramidal cells of the motor cortex discharge impulses down the pyramidal tract to motoneurons in the spinal cord that control movement. But this is only the last stage in the brain events concerned in voluntary movement. There are fundamental problems. In the initiation of a voluntary movement by a motive/intention, what are the sequences of events being set up in the brain?

A remarkable series of experiments in the last few years has transformed our understanding of the cerebral events concerned with the initiation of a voluntary movement. It can now be stated that the first brain reactions caused by the intention to move are in nerve cells of the supplementary motor area (SMA). It is right at the top of the brain. This area was recognized by the renowned neurosurgeon, Wilder Penfield, when he was stimulating the exposed human brain in the search for epileptic "foci" (regions of aberrant activity associated with epileptic seizures). Stimulation of this area did not cause sharply localized responses for the motor cortex. Instead there were writing or adversive movements of large parts of the torso and limbs, even of the same side, and also incoherent vocalizations. So this area was neglected for decades as it did not seem to have an interesting function. Now, from this Cinderella status, the SMA has been advanced to a role of higher interest.

There is strong support for the hypothesis that the SMA is the sole recipient area of the brain for mental intentions that lead to voluntary movements. This is a most important improvement on the concept that the mental act of intention to move was widely dispersed in its action on the brain. Such a sharp focusing lends precision to our attempts to define the manner in which some particular voluntary action is brought about. The concept of motor programs is important in this enterprise. Instead of just waving our arms or indulging in some other crude movement to display intention leading to action, we have to recognize the complexity of the muscle actions in bringing about any skilled and learned movement. It can be as commonplace as extending one's hand to pick up a cup, and, in an elegant and smooth action, to bring the cup to one's lips for a drink, thereafter placing the cup back in its saucer. A most complex series of movements has been accomplished, each of which can be reduced to some constituent motor programs: putting one's hand to the cup; securely grasping the handle; smoothly lifting the cup; bringing it correctly to the lips; drinking, which is a whole series of lip, tongue, pharyngeal and swallowing movements; and finally the return of the cup. Thus there is a whole interlocking series of movements involving contraction of a large number of muscles, all nicely graded and sequenced. It is convenient to describe this complex movement as being composed of a harmony of elemental motor programs.

Let us consider how our intention to enact such a voluntary movement can be related to the role of the SMA as the mediator between the mental act of intention and the assemblage of motor programs involved in the voluntary movement. We must first postulate that the mental intention acts on the SMA in a highly selective way, and that the SMA contains, as it were, an inventory of all the learned motor programs. This immense stored repertoire of the learned motor programs of a lifetime could not be stored in the SMA, which is a quite limited area of the cerebral cortex with perhaps 50 million neurons and 15,000 modules on each side. All that is necessary is for the SMA to contain the inventory of the motor programs; an inventory which comprises addresses to the storage bank of the motor programs. The SMA is known to have major lines of communication to the presumed storage sites in the cerebral cortex (particularly the premotor cortex and in the basal ganglia and the cerebellum). By radio-tracer techniques these areas have been shown to be called into action in voluntary movements, and many nerve cells in these circuits have been shown to be active before the discharge of the motor cortical cells.

Thus we have in outline a hypothesis of how the mental act of intention can, by action through the SMA, bring about the desired movement.

Let us now return to the performance of the nerve cells of the SMA in a voluntary act. A single nerve cell under observation will be firing at the usual slow and irregular frequency, the background discharge. Then there is a sharp increase of the frequency of firing and in a little more than a fifth of a second the movement starts. We could in fact predict the onset of the movement from the observed discharges of the nerve cell. It is important to recognize that this burst of discharge of the observed SMA cell was not triggered by some other nerve cell of the SMA or elsewhere in the brain. The first discharges occur in the SMA.

So we have here an irrefutable demonstration that a mental act of intention initiates the burst of discharges of a nerve cell. Furthermore, when hundreds of SMA nerve cells are observed, only some are activated at this early stage. Others come later; others may fire in two successive bursts; still others are even silenced. And these specific types of response are repeatedly displayed by any nerve cell in relation to a particular voluntary act. Thus we have to postulate that the mental act of intention was being effective in a discriminating fashion. There was observed in fact a most complex pattern of neuronal responses of the SMA nerve cells. So the mental act of intention is exerted in a subtle discriminating fashion on the constituent nerve cells of the SMAs on each side.

It is evident that we have embarked upon a temerarious field of speculation. But the fact remains that skilled and learned movements are carried out at will; that immensely complicated neural machinery is necessary for any such act; and that the mental influences must work in a coded manner on the SMA neurons and generate corresponding codes of spatiotemporal patterns in the discharges of the SMA neurons. Each such pattern presumably is an inventory of motor programs with the addresses for transmitting the codes so as to institute the activities of these motor programs.

How can the mental act of intention activate across the mind-brain frontier those particular SMA neurons in the appropriate code for activating the motor programs that bring about intended voluntary movements? The answer is that, despite the so-called "insuperable" difficulty of having a non-material mind act on a material brain, it has been demonstrated to occur by a mental intention, no doubt to the great discomfiture of all materialists and physicalists.

## Dr. Sperry

Permit me to draw attention to some rather familiar experiences of the distinction between brain dynamics and inner mental experience. For simplicity, consider an elemental subjective sensation—and for reasons that will become evident, let us use the sensation of pain instead of philosophy's old favorite, the color red. More specifically, make it pain in the wrist and fingers of the left hand of an arm that was amputated above the elbow some months previously. Suffering caused by pain localized in a phantom limb is no easier to bear than if the limb was still there. It is easier, however, with the example, to infer where our conscious awareness must reside.

With regard to this conscious sensation of pain, the contention is that any groans it may evoke—and any other response measures the patient may take as a result of the pain sensation—are indeed caused, not by the biophysics, chemistry, or physiology of the cerebral nerve impulses as such, but by the pain quality, the pain property, per se. This brings us to the real crux of the argument. Nerve excitations are just as common to pleasure, of course, as to pain, or any other sensation. What is critical is the unique patterning of cerebral excitation that produces pain instead of something else. It is the overall functional property of this pain pattern that is critical in the causal sequence of brain affairs. This pattern has a dynamic entity, the qualitative effect of which must be conceived functionally and operationally, and in terms of its impact on a living, unanesthetized cerebral system. This overall pattern effect in brain dynamics is the pain quality of inner experience.

Above simple pain and other elemental sensations in brain dynamics, we find, of course, the more complex but equally potent forces of perception, emotion, reason, belief, insight, judgment and cognition. In the onward flow of conscious brain states, one state calling up the next, these are the kinds of dynamic entities that call the plays.

It is exactly these encompassing mental forces that direct and govern the inner flow patterns of impulse traffic, including their physiological, electro-chemical, atomic, subatomic, and subnuclear details. It is important to remember in this connection that all of the simpler, more primitive, elemental forces remain present and operative; none has been canceled. These lower-level forces and properties, however, have been superseded in successive steps, encompassed or enveloped as it were, by those forces of increasingly complex organizational entities. For the transmission of nerve impulses, all of the usual electrical, chemical, and physiological laws apply, of course, at the level of cell, fiber and synaptic junction. Proper function in the uppermost levels depends to a large extent upon normal operation at the subsidiary levels. It is a special characteristic of these larger functional patterns in the brain, however, that they have a coherence and organization that enables them to carry on orderly function in the presence of considerable disruptive damage in the lower-level components.

Near the apex of this compound command system in the brain we find ideas. In the brain model proposed here, the causal potency of an idea, or an ideal, becomes just as real as that of a molecule, a cell, or a nerve impulse. Ideas cause ideas and help evolve new ideas. They interact with each other and with other mental forces in the same brain, in neighboring brains, and in distant, foreign brains. And they also interact with real consequence upon the external surroundings to produce *in toto* an explosive advance in evolution on this globe far beyond anything known before, including the emergence of the living cell.

# *Episteme*

## DONALD E. POLKINGHORNE

*Dr. Polkinghorne is
past president of Saybrook Institute and is now professor
of counseling, school of psychology at the California
State University, Fullerton. He has contributed many
articles to learned journals. Among his books are
**Methodology for the Human Sciences** and
**Narrative Knowing and the Human Sciences**.*

A new conversation has emerged which provides a fresh set of concepts and assumptions in which discussions about knowledge can take place. The new conversation is called "epistemic" and it is replacing the previous conversation call "epistemological." The "epistemological" conversation originated with the Enlightenment and its focus was on how true and certain knowledge could be produced. The "epistemic" conversation originated with the post-structuralists and its focus is on how humans construct interpretations and understandings which are useful and dependable.

In the "epistemological" conversation, discussants assume that knowledge is a true representation of reality as it is independent of knowers. In the "epistemic" conversation, discussants assume that knowledge is a cultural production linked to one's cultural metanarrative. A metanarrative is the basic story in which a culture's values, aspirations, and social rules are expressed. Epistemic knowledge is always under development; it is a perpetually unfinished tool whose function is to assist in achieving cultural goals. Thus, in the epistemic conversation, the producers of knowledge need to be concerned with the social use of the knowledge they develop; the knowledge they develop cannot be divorced from social values. In addition, although the producers attempt to achieve the most reliable understandings possible, they realize that knowledge is always unfinished and open to revision.

The epistemic conversation does not cohere around a single issue. Rather a variety of themes receive attention. One theme is the expansion of the notion of rationality from an adherence to the deductive thought of formal logic to the inclusion of the range of thought processes humans use to make sense of their interaction with the world, one another, and themselves. Another theme is the expansion of the aims of knowledge from an exclusive interest with the natural laws which govern the material realm to a concern with understanding the human dimensions of beauty, values, and wisdom.

The epistemic conversation takes place in a context that acknowledges that our knowledge of the universe is developed according to models and metaphors. These mental pictures help order our perceptions and actions, but they are not mirror images of reality. Reality itself is not constructed in conformity with any model we have of it. For example, reality is not logical in the manner in which we think when using formal logic. The image of the real is not one of a single unified structure, but rather a collage, consisting of various systems with multiple organizing principles. The systems unfold according to varying temporal patterns and are affected by interaction with each other according to their own internal structures. The concept that the multiple manifestations of reality operate according to only one principle or are determined by one mathematical or machine-like pattern is seen by the post-structuralists in the conversation as the result of the human desire to see unity.

Some participants view Nietzsche's ideas as an anticipation of the epistemic conversation. Nietzsche looked at the world in general as if it were a sort of artwork; in particular, as if it were a literary text in the process of being read. Many of his views of the natural and human realms are developed by generalizing to them ideas and principles that would normally apply to reading literary texts and their characters. He understood that the world was aesthetically self-creating, self-read, instead of being a determinate manifestation of formal logic. Nietzsche attributes to art an ontogenetic, that is, a world making significance. In his view, the world in which we live is a work of art that is continually being created and re-created, and there is nothing either behind or beyond giving it form. Heidegger expanded the notion of art to include in it the use of language in general, reading in particular. For him language has the power to provide an opening in which reality shows itself.

Interpretations of the natural and human realms need to assume an aesthetic approach into order to provide a fuller openness and better fit to that which knowledge seeks to expose. The use of models and metaphors in the ways we make our pictures of the world are appropriate. Nietzsche values art because it is non-conceptual, and is a recognition that we know only the semblance of reality, not reality itself. He envisioned a reunification of the "artistic energies and the practical wisdom of life" with scientific thinking.

The appreciation that knowledge is aesthetic in form is a significant change from the traditional view in which art has "no commerce with epistemology." The aesthetic form was understood to be a self-enclosed domain, without relation to knowledge or truth. In this view, whose genealogy is usually traced back to Kant, art is a recreation, a playfulness that contrasts with the "real" world of work. The aesthetic mode was subjective or psychological rather than cognitive in its focus, since it was understood to function in relation to a feeling or state of mind (in Kant's case, the "disinterested pleasure" that art induces), and not in relation to a truth-claim. Opposed to the "psychological" view is the "ontological" view, which holds that the aesthetic mode is not mere play but can be a disclosure of truth.

The epistemic conversation emphasizes the logic of difference rather than the Enlightenment logic of identity. In the logic of identity the importance of an object or event is understood to be the properties it has in common with other objects in the same category. The logic of difference focuses on the properties unique to the individual object or event. For example, in looking at a table, the logic of identity would look toward the aspects of the particular table that are the same as other tables, four legs, a flat surface and height, and sets it apart from other categories, such as a bench.

The logic of difference is concerned to note the features which make it this table and no other, its color, shape of its legs, position within a particular room, the period of time in which it exists. The metaphorical property of language notes that objects have similarities as well as dissimilarities. The conversation holds that the more significant meanings of an object are found in its dissimilarity than in its similarity.

Formal reasoning selects for study the general and similarities within categories and gains knowledge of what is approximate and the same, but loses the information of difference and uniqueness. Epistemic reasoning focuses on the surface and draws out the information that makes the object distinct.

The new conversation locates the dimension of time as primary. In opposition to the search for the unchanging and permanent, it highlights change and temporality as the most basic feature of the real. Both the natural and human realms are defined temporally. The narrative form of presentation is used to describe the temporal relationships that hold between events and objects. The participants do not accept the notion put forward by Hegel and Marx that history is the unfolding of some underlying pattern of development. Rather they use genealogy as a method to reveal the discontinuity between events as opposed to a continuous single scheme of development. Foucault uses the term episteme to refer to the set of relations that unite the discursive practices of a given period. I have used the term "conversation" in a similar way to point to the differences in possible discussions about the nature of human science. Genealogy also exposes the origins from which emerged the views that have become sedimented and accepted as truths. Having an origin is being part of history, and this implies that views are not permanent and it is possible for them to come to an end.

The old, epistemological, conversation, par excellence between author and reader, was an attempt to uncover a Man or Culture or Nature or History underlying the flux of surface experience. The postmodern discussion values and studies that which appears. Rather than attempting to delve beneath the formal surface of logic to its deep structures and laws, it seeks to describe the nuances and fullness of that which is directly present. What is experienced is not looked through as if it were a mere instance of some pattern or principle, but it becomes the focal point for understanding. Science is descriptive of appearances rather than explanations of them, and its descriptions seek irregularities as well as the regularities. The format of description emphasizes the idea of horizon which extends beyond the event rather than the concept of which the event is an instance. The goal of knowledge is not a theoretical system that describes the laws and rules that govern events, but a full description of events in their temporal relationships.

Of special concern to the epistemic conversation is to overcome the separation and ultimate dismissal of moral judgments from the realm of knowledge. In spite of the recognition that knowledge is relative to knower and culture, participants of the conversation are aware that humans still engage in choices and involvement in the world. In making his threefold division of knowledge, Kant suggested that literature might be the realm in which science and morality are brought together. Heidegger suggested that theoretical and practical knowledge were drawn from a more "essential ground" or "essential thinking" that is aesthetic, that is, created within the reader or viewer. McIntrye has suggested that the understanding of action and value be approached through the aesthetic form of narrative. The goal of the epistemic conversation is to explore the kind of knowledge that will give more than technical skill and competence for manipulating and controlling nature and people for some national or corporate end. It seeks to develop a human science that would concern itself with capacity to make judgments that are based on appreciation of the natural and human realms as well as informed by technical information, that is, it seeks to address the issue of human wisdom.

# 4 *Reading And Society*

# The Meaning of
# Imagination

MARTYN GOFF

*Martyn Goff, OBE,
was chief executive of The Queen's Book Trust in
London for many years until his recent retirement.
The Queen's Book Trust has become internationally
famous for its cultural successes in fostering
reading. Mr. Goff has been asked by the governments
of the United States and of Germany to consult
with them on literacy programs; he is now
chairman of Henry Sotheran Limited.*

When Jacobo Timmermans, a prominent South American newspaper owner and book publisher, was released from prison, a sentence that included torture and great hardship, he was taken before the country's dictator prior to being deported. A brazen man, he asked the dictator why, when he had daily published a newspaper critical of "the great man" and nothing had happened to him, he had been thrown in prison for publishing a book containing similar material.

"Because," answered the dictator, "a book has a life of its own, a newspaper can be silenced, confiscated, pressured or won over with threats. If the journalist's articles are not published, their writing has no importance. Furthermore, if they are not going to be published, they won't get written in the first place. But books are written, whether they are published at the moment or in the place they are written. They have a secure destiny, a manifest destiny, a lasting experience."

Books are not only essential to all of us as individuals but also to us as a society. As Barbara Tuchman said in a lecture to the Center for the Book at the Library of Congress in October 1979:

> The essential nature of TV is that its program is designed not for self-expression but to sell something other than itself to the greatest number of viewers. Books being self-selected by the consumer, can keep pace with his growing maturity in age and taste, whereas the media on the whole must remain at a level that its programmers believe palatable to the widest possible audience . . . Books by their heterogeneity can never represent a managed culture, whereas the airwaves by their nature are controlled by licensing might.

I suspect that those two quotations make the case for the book very strongly, but in case I am left even with a single doubter, let me add some very different but telling quotations from Margaret Meek, that expert in the field of children's books:

> Can you really imagine what life would be like if you had never learned to read? The special disadvantages are easy to understand. But what about encounters with new ideas?

What a horrifying thought!—to be cut off from new lines of ideas and thought through not being able to read. Yet according to Kozol there are 22,000,000 functional illiterates in America, 22,000,000 who cannot read the POISON warning on an aerosol can of pesticide!

Margaret Meek again:

> To be literate in the civic or material sense of belonging to a literate society is to be able not only to read but also to question the authority of even the most official-looking document that makes demands on us.

Finally, from the same source:

> It is also important to realize that not all the electronic media in the world will replace what happens when a reader meets a writer. Reading is the active encounter of one mind and one imagination with another. Talk happens; the words fly, remembered or not. Writing remains; we read it at our own pace which is the rate of our thinking. Reading cannot be done without thought. As it is a kind of inner speech, it is bound to have a marked effect on the growth of the mind of the reader.

I hope that makes my case for the book. But if you are already thinking that surely some of the other media can do much the same, my answer is no. The key factor about the book against the TV programme or video is that the book alone requires the active participation of the reader. The other media wash over or through him, failing to activate his imagination, and, often, his brain.

If I were to show an audience a movie with Elizabeth Taylor and Richard Burton playing the two main roles, all of them would see exactly the same two people, the same created characters. But if they were all to read the book from which the movie is taken, then each one of them would flesh out the characters slightly differently; or, in other words, their brains would have to be active in providing the flesh for the author's bones.

A further advantage of the book is serendipity; we go to look up a word in a dictionary and learn five other words on the way. When I was at college a teacher told me to read an essay by E. M. Forster. It was quite a good essay, too. But, thumbing through the rest of the book, I chanced upon Two Cheers for Democracy; and that essay of Forster's had a profound effect on me, an effect that has lasted until this day.

If we move from the general to the particular, then books have even more advantages. Let me illustrate this with a few random choices.

I had been to Africa about ten times when I chanced upon Patrick Marnham's *Fantastic Invasion* (published later as a Penguin under the title *African Despatches*). It changed my whole perception of Africa not only politically, though that above all, but even in the matter of National Parks. Like most people I had thought these wholly good. Marnham showed me that their interference with nature can also be harmful and lead to more, not less, animals being extinguished! Or what about a recent novel, Margaret Atwood's *Handmaid's Tale*, as a remarkable piece of imaginative, futuristic fiction? In painting a new—and very grim—world of the future, she illuminates so much of our world, the world we are at present living in. We are given an experience that is difficult to forget or bury.

The Deputy Director of Book Promotion of UNESCO was surprised that I travelled in Africa and elsewhere without a very high grade shortwave radio. "How else do you know what's going on in the world when you're in far flung places or behind the Iron Curtain?" So I bought a Sony ICF 7600D. With it I have only to key in the wavelength to its computer for that station to appear like magic. Or I can go to sleep listening to one programme with the radio turning itself off after half an hour and wake up to another which I have programmed for the morning. For me it is the ultimate in the new technology. Except. . .that I had to master an eighty page handbook before I could as much as turn the set on!

In 1979 Dr. Christopher Evans in his book, *The Mighty Micro* wrote:

> In sum the 1980s will see the book as we know it, and as our ancestor's created and cherished it, begin a slow but steady decline into oblivion.

Much of the early chapters of that book are in similar vein, though it is worth noting that on the back of the jacket Dr. Evans was photographed in a booklined study!

Of course Dr. Evans had been preceded by Marshall McLuhan by some years, the same Professor McLuhan who foretold the end of the book for after all "the medium is the message."

Dr. Evans' 1980s are over, and the number of books published and sold is increasing everywhere. Marshall McLuhan, in a letter to me only months before his death, wrote:

> There have been indications of TV saturation among high school students. That tends to mean they have undergone considerable depletion of psychic resources before reaching this state of apathy.

A little further on in the same letter:

> The main effect of television is loss of identity and its ensuing violence.

My message is that the book is not only going to survive the coming of the new technology but continue to grow in importance. I base such a bold statement not on Dr. Evans having clearly been wrong in his time scale, nor on Marshall McLuhan's retraction of his former beliefs. My reasons for believing in the future of the book are wider and more complex than those two simple facts.

Perhaps first we can deal with the prophets of doom who always see every new invention as incorporating a death sentence on its predecessors. Dan Boorstine, the former Librarian of Congress, has shown us quite clearly that, whereas new art forms and new means of retrieving information are always initially seem as dispossessing their forerunners, they almost always end only by modifying them. For example, the coming of photography was seen as the end of painting. But what happened was that by largely removing from painting its principal task of recording faces, groups, houses, ships and so on—it freed that art in a way that led to abstract painting, surrealism, cubism, vorticism and the like. Painting is as strong today as ever, even though photography itself is now considered an art form.

Similarly the gramophone record was seen as the end of live concert, whereas it turned out to be the biggest advertisement for such concerts. Records converted millions to music and still left those millions wanting to hear their favorite artists in the flesh. Radio was to have been the end of newspapers and then itself was going to be superseded by the arrival of television. But newspapers are alive and fairly healthy —at least in circulation figures—despite both those media of communication; and radio has blossomed into all sorts of new fields; local stations, CB radio and the like. The relation of newspapers on the one hand and TV and radio on the other is a clue to the importance of the written word. We see an item of news on the television or hear about it on the radio, but for deeper, considered views—for *knowledge* as against *information*—we turn to our newspapers where those items are analyzed for us in depth—at least in *The Times* and *Guardian*, if not in the *Sun*.

So there is no logical step whereby the arrival of television and computers and video recorders will put an end to the book. For obviously while much information retrieval will be switched to those new technologies, the technologies themselves need accompanying books.

There are also a number of practical reasons why the book will stay. First, the book is cheap. Before anyone starts to complain that a biography can cost between 15 and 25 pounds, notice that whereas that sort of sum spent on a meal is soon forgotten, the book is always there to be read, which may be an eight to ten hour experience; re-read; lent to someone else or to many others and, if returned, put on a shelf to become one of the most delightful forms of furniture and decoration.

Secondly, the book is amazingly portable. It can be carried anywhere: on a train, a plane, on the beach, in a park, into a bath. Now in some of those places you can take a radio or portable TV, or even a tape recorder, but not by any means all.

Thirdly, a book is flexible. You can fail to get the meaning of a sentence; put your finger or a bit of paper in that page and read on, flick back and forth between that and other pages until the meaning becomes clear. And you can do it a thousand times more easily than the same operation with a tape or video cassette.

Fourthly, book reading is wonderfully private. If just one person in a room switches on a hi-fi or TV set, everyone's aural attention is trespassed upon. But dozens of people in a room can be reading a different book at the same moment without disturbing anyone else.

But these are minor, practical advantages. However real they may be, they are not why the book will continue to exist alongside the new technologies. So let us begin to look at some of the deeper implications of the continuing importance of the book.

First, a minor one. George Steiner once said: "I go into a bookshop for the book I didn't know I wanted." In the same way when we look up a word in a dictionary, we chance on and learn another half a dozen words that we were not previously familiar with. This form of serendipity is a painless and pleasant way of acquiring knowledge.

Second, we read a book at our own pace, not that of the film or television producer. As Barbara Tuchman made clear in the passage quoted earlier, everyone can read the same book at a different pace. In transmitted programmes the pace is dictated and is often set at the level of the lowest. More importantly, the new technologies can be controlled in a way that is impossible via the book. "Books," if I may repeat the quote: "can never represent a managed culture."

Every day we come across some extraordinary new example of contemporary technology. A telephone that tells a retailer whether a customer's credit card can be used for a given sum if the card is dropped into a slot in the phone and a certain number dialled; an on-line computer that tells us how many free seats there are in an aircraft still 7,000 miles away; a light pen that reads a minute ticket on an object being sold and alters stock records and re-orders instantly. And yet . . . the people operating these modern marvels are every bit as liable to misunderstandings with their colleagues as were their predecessors in the steam age. Those misunderstandings arise from an imprecise or ambivalent use of words.

For words remain the way in which we talk to each other, inform each other, programme each other; and words are learnt and understood, words are *felt*, by reading.

I have left till last one branch of the book that has a function in our society of the greatest importance, on which, in the face of a world seemingly hell-bent on its own destruction, becomes more important as day succeeds day.

I refer, of course, to Literature. Long after we have forgotten the names of the Presidents and Prime Ministers,

Kings and Queens, those of the greatest artistic creators
remain household words. Who was the Elector of Bavaria in
Beethoven's time? Or the Queen in Shakespeare's? If the Arts
are one of the few glories of mankind, then Literature shares
with Music and Painting the forefront. Our writers are as vital
to society as ever they were. Over sixty years ago R. G.
Collingwood wrote:

> The artist must prophesy, not in the sense that he foretells
> things to come, but in the sense that he tells his audience,
> at the risk of their displeasure, the secrets of their own
> hearts. His business as an artist is to speak out, to make a
> clean breast. But what he has to utter is not, as the indi-
> vidualistic theory of art would have us think, his own
> secrets. As spokesman of his community, the secrets he
> must utter are theirs. The reason why they need him is
> that no community altogether knows its own heart; and
> by failing in this knowledge a community deceives itself
> on the one subject concerning which ignorance means
> death. For the evils which come from that ignorance the
> poet as prophet suggests no remedy, because he has
> already given one. The remedy is the poem itself. Art is
> the community's medicine for the worst disease of the
> mind, the corruption of consciousness.

We plunge headlong into one piece of new technology
after another. We do not stop to consider the consequences.
No one invented the aeroplane in order to transport bombs or
nuclear weapons, but that is what it now does. No one
invented children's television programmes to damage children's concentration, but that is what it now does. The attention span of the average child is dropping fast, because of
television. The child now requires instant attraction or the set
is switched off. The same shortened attention span is brought
to books.

We have a huge task to give the book back the priority it should have, above all for children. We must cease to regard reading for children as a middle class thing. We must use books that appeal across the whole ethnic spectrum as if such an approach was entirely natural and logical, which it is. We must convince children that books are as much fun as anything else. We must remember that books are one of the finest ingredients of our history and lives; and act accordingly.

# *The Modern Conscience*

## NAGUIB MAHFOUZ

*Naguib Mahfouz is
the premier novelist of the Arab world. He has written
more than 30 novels, and each of his new books is
regarded as a major cultural event in Egypt,
his native country. He received the Nobel Prize
for Literature in 1988.*

. . .

I am the son of two civilizations that at a certain age in history have formed a happy marriage. The first of these, seven thousand years old, is the Pharaonic civilization; the second, one thousand four hundred years old, is the Islamic one. I am perhaps in no need to introduce to any of you either of the two, you being the elite, the learned ones. But there is no harm, in our present situation of acquaintance and communion, in a mere reminder.

As for Pharaonic civilization I will not talk of the conquests and the building of empires. This has become a worn out pride the mention of which modern conscience, thank God, feels uneasy about. Nor will I talk about how it was guided for the first time to the existence of God and its ushering in the dawn of human conscience. This is a long history and there is not one of you who is not acquainted with the prophet-king Akhenaton. I will not even speak of this civilization's achievements in art and literature, and its renowned miracles: the Pyramids and the Sphinx and Karnak. For he who has not had the chance to see these monuments has read about them and pondered over their forms.

Let me, then, introduce Pharaonic civilization with what seems like a story since my personal circumstances have ordained that I become a storyteller. Hear, then, this recorded historical incident: Old papyri relate that Pharaoh had learned of the existence of a sinful relation between some women of the harem and men of his court. It was expected that he should finish them off in accordance with the spirit of his time. But he, instead, called to his presence the choice men of law and asked them to investigate what he has come to learn. He told them that he wanted the Truth so that he could pass his sentence with Justice.

This conduct, in my opinion, is greater than founding an empire or building the Pyramids. It is more telling of the superiority of that civilization than any riches or splendour. Gone

now is that civilization—a mere story of the past. One day the
great Pyramid will disappear too. But Truth and Justice will
remain for as long as Mankind has a ruminative mind and a
living conscience.

As for Islamic civilization I will not talk about its call for
the establishment of a union between all Mankind under the
guardianship of the Creator, based on freedom, equality and
forgiveness. Nor will I talk about the greatness of its prophet.
For among your thinkers there are those who regard him the
greatest man in history. I will not talk of its conquests which
have planted thousands of minarets calling for worship,
devoutness and good throughout great expanses of land from
the environs of India and China to the boundaries of France.
Nor will I talk of the fraternity between religions and races that
has been achieved in its embrace in a spirit of tolerance
unknown to Mankind neither before nor since.

I will, instead, introduce that civilization in a moving dramatic situation summarizing one of its most conspicuous traits:
In one victorious battle against Byzantium it has given back its
prisoners of war in return for a number of books of the ancient
Greek heritage in philosophy, medicine and mathematics. This
is a testimony of value for the human spirit in its demand for
knowledge, even though the demander was a believer in God
and the demanded a fruit of a pagan civilization.

It was my fate to be born in the lap of these two civilizations, and to absorb their milk, to feed on their literature
and art. Then I drank the nectar of your rich and fascinating
culture. From the inspiration of all this—as well as my own
anxieties—words bedewed from me.

. . .

You may be wondering: This man coming from the third
world, how did he find the peace of mind to write stories? You
are perfectly right. I come from a world labouring under the
burden of debts whose paying back exposes it to starvation or
very close to it. Some of its people perish in Asia from floods,

others do so in Africa from famine. In South Africa millions have been undone with rejection and with deprivation of all human rights in the age of human rights, as though they were not counted among humans. In the West Bank and Gaza there are people who are lost in spite of the fact that they are living on their own land, land of their fathers, grandfathers and great grandfathers. They have risen to demand the first right secured by primitive Man; namely, that they should have their proper place recognized by others as their own. They were paid back for their brave and noble move—men, women, youths and children alike—by the breaking of bones, killing with bullets, destroying of houses and torture in prisons and camps. Surrounding them are 150 million Arabs following what is happening in anger and grief. This threatens the area with a disaster if it is not saved by the wisdom of those desirous of a just and comprehensive peace.

Yes, how did the man coming from the Third World find peace of mind to write stories? Fortunately, art is generous and sympathetic. In the same way that it dwells with the happy ones it does not desert the wretched. It offers both alike the convenient means for expressing what swells up in their bosom.

In this decisive moment in the history of civilization it is inconceivable and unacceptable that the moans of Mankind should die out in the void. There is no doubt that Mankind has at last come of age, and our era carries the expectations of *entente* between the Super Powers. The human mind now assumes the task of eliminating all causes of destruction and annihilation. And just as scientists exert themselves to cleanse the environment of industrial pollution, intellectuals ought to exert themselves to cleanse humanity of moral pollution. It is both our right and duty to demand of the big leaders in the countries of civilization as well as their economists to affect a real leap that would place them into the focus of the age.

In the olden times every leader worked for the good of his own nation alone. The others were considered adversaries, or subjects of exploitation. There was no regard to any value but that of superiority and personal glory. For the sake of this, many morals, ideals and values were wasted; many unethical means were justified; many uncounted souls were made to perish. Lies, deceit, treachery, cruelty reigned as the signs of sagacity and the proof of greatness. Today, this view needs to be changed from its very source. Today, the greatness of a civilized leader ought to be measured by the universality of his vision and his sense of responsibility towards all humankind.

. . .

# *Reading in the Third World*

WOLE SOYINKA

*Wole Soyinka,
a Nigerian, has lived and taught in that country after
havng been educated in Great Britain. He was
the 1986 recipient of the Nobel Prize for Literature.
Dr. Soyinka has published more than
twenty works of drama, novels and poetry
but is best known as a dramatist.*

. . .

J ack Cope surely sums it up in his foreword to
*The Adversary Within*, a study of dissidence in Afrikaaner literature when he states:

"Looking back from the perspective of the present, I think
it can justly be said that, at the core of the matter, the
Afrikaaner leaders in 1924 took the wrong turning. Themselves the victims of imperialism in its most evil aspect,
all their sufferings and enormous loss of life nevertheless
failed to convey to them the obvious historical lesson.
They became themselves the new imperialists. They took
over from Britain the mantle of empire and colonialism.
They could well have set their faces against annexation,
aggression, colonial exploitation, and oppression, racial
arrogance and barefaced hypocrisy, of which they had
been themselves the victims. They could have opened the
doors to humane ideas and civilizing processes and
transformed the great territory with its incalculable
resources into another New World. Instead they deliber-
ately set the clock back where ever they could. Taking
over ten million indigenous subjects from British colonial
rule, they stripped them of what limited rights they had
gained over a century and tightened the screws on their
subjection."

Well, perhaps the wars against Chaka and Dingaan and
Diginswayo, even the Great Trek were then too fresh in *laager
memory*. But we are saying that over a century has passed since
then, a century in which the world has leapt, in comparative
tempo with the past, at least three centuries. And we have seen
the potential of man and woman—of all races—contend with
the most jealously guarded sovereignty of Nature and the
Cosmos. In every field, both in the Humanitites and Sciences,
we have seen that human creativity has confronted and

tempered the hostility of his environment, adapting, moderating, converting, harmonizing, and even subjugating. Triumphing over errors and resuming the surrendered fields, man has had time to lick his wounds and listen again to the urgings of his spirit. History—distorted, opportunistic renderings of history have been cleansed and restored to truthful reality, because the traducers of the history of others have discovered that the further they advanced, the more their very progress was checked and vitiated by the lacunae they had purposefully inserted in the history of others. Self-interest dictated yet another round of revisionism—slight, niggardly concessions to begin with. But a breach had been made in the dam and an avalanche proved the logical progression. From the heart of jungles, even before the aid of high-precision cameras mounted on orbiting satellites, civilizations have resurrected, documenting their own existence with unassailable iconography and art. More amazing still, the records of the ancient voyagers, the merchant adventurers of the age when Europe did not yet require to dominate territories in order to feed its industrial mills—those objective recitals of mariners and adventurers from antiquity confirmed what the archeological remains affirmed so loudly. They spoke of living communities which regulated their own lives, which had evolved a working relationship with Nature, which ministered to their own wants and secured their future with their own genius. These narratives, uncluttered by the impure motives which needed to mystify the plain self-serving rush to dismantle independent societies for easy plundering—pointed accusing fingers unerringly in the direction of European savants, philosophers, scientists, and theorists of human evolution. Gobineau is a notorious name, but how many students of European thought today, even among us Africans, recall that several of the most revered names in European philosophy—Hegel, Locke, Montesquieu, Hume, Voltaire—an endless list—were unabashed theorists of racial superiority and denigrators of the African history and being. As for the more prominent names among the theorists of revolution and class struggle—we will draw the curtain of extenuation on their own intellectual aberration, forgiving them a little for their vision of an end to human exploitation.

. . .

Indeed it is probably even more pertinent to remind this racist society that our African world, its cultural hoards and philosophical thought, have had concrete impacts on the racists' own forebears, have proved seminal to a number of movements and even created tributaries, both pure and polluted, among the white indigenes in their own homelands.

Such a variety of encounters and responses have been due, naturally, to profound searches for new directions in their cultural adventures, seeking solaces to counter the remorseless mechanization of their existence, indeed seeking new meanings for the mystery of life and attempting to overcome the social malaise created by the very triumphs of their own civilization. It has created in places a near-deification of the African person—that phase in which every African had to be a prince—which yet again, was coupled with a primitive fear and loathing for the person of the African. To these paradoxical responses, the essentiality of our black being remains untouched. For the black race knows, and is content simply to know, itself. It is the European world that has sought, with the utmost zeal, to redefine itself through these encounters, even when it does appear that he is endeavouring to grant meaning to an experience of the African world.

We can make use of the example of that period of European Expressionism, a movement which saw African art, music, and dramatic rituals share the same sphere of influence as the most disparate, astonishingly incompatible collection of ideas, ideologies, and social tendencies—Freud, Karl Marx, Bakunin, Nietzsche, cocaine, and free love. What wonder then, that the spiritual and plastic presences of the Bakota, Nimba, the Yoruba, Dogon, Dan etc., should *find themselves at once the inspiration* and the anathematized of a delirium that was most peculiarly European, mostly Teutonic and Gallic, spanning at least four decades across the last and the present centuries. Yet the vibrant goal remained the complete liberation of man, that freeing of his yet untapped potential that would carve marble blocks for the constructing of a new world, debourgeoisify existing constrictions of European thought and light the flame to form a new fraternity throughout this brave new world. Yes, within this single movement that covered the vast spectrum of outright fascism, anarchism, and revolutionary communism, the reality that was Africa was, as always, sniffed at, delicately tested, swallowed entire, regurgitated, appropriated, extoiled, and damned in the revelatory frenzy of a continent's recreative energies.

. . .

There are, after all, European nations today whose memory of domination by other races remains so vivid more than two centuries after liberation, that a terrible vengeance culturally, socially, and politically is still exacted, even at this very moment, from the descendants of those erstwhile conquerors. I have visited such nations whose cruel histories under foreign domination are enshrined as icons to daily consciousness in monuments, parks, in museums and churches, in documentation, woodcuts, and photogravures displayed under bullet-proof glass-cases but, most telling of all, is the reduction of the remnants of the conquering hordes to the degraded status of aliens on sufferance, with reduced civic rights, privileges, and social status, a barely tolerate marginality that expresses itself in the pathos of downcast faces, dropped shoulders, and apologetic encounters in those rare times when intercourse with the latterly assertive race is unavoidable. Yes, all this I have seen, and much of it has been written about and debated in international gatherings. And even while acknowledging the poetic justice of it in the abstract, one cannot help but wonder if a physical pound of

flesh, excised at birth, is not a kinder act than a lifelong visita-
tion of the sins of the father on the sons even to the tenth and
twelfth generations.

Confronted with such traditions of attenuating the racial
and cultural pride of these marginalized or minority peoples,
the mind travels back to our own societies where such
causative histories are far fresher in the memory, where the
ruins of formerly thriving communities still speak eloquent
accusations and the fumes still rise from the scorched earth
strategies of colonial and racist myopia. Yet the streets bear the
names of former oppressors, their statues and other symbols of
subjugation are left to decorate their squares, the consciousness
of a fully confident people having relegated them to mere
decorations and roosting-places for bats and pigeons. And the
libraries remain unpurged, so that new generations freely
browse though the works of Frobenius, of Hume, Hegel, or
Montesquieu and others without first encountering, freshly
stamped on the fly-leaf: WARNING! THIS WORK IS
DANGEROUS FOR YOUR RACIAL SELF-ESTEEM.

Yet these proofs of accommodation, on the grand or
minuscule scale, collective, institutional, or individual, must
not be taken as proof of an infinite, uncritical capacity of black
patience. They constitute in their own nature, a body of tests,
an accumulation of debt, an implicit offer that must be
matched by concrete returns. They are the blocks in a suspended bridge begun from one end of a chasm which, whether
the builders will it or not, must obey the law of matter and
crash down beyond a certain point, settling definitively into
the widening chasm of suspicion, frustration, and redoubled
hate. On that testing ground which, for us, is Southern Africa,
that medieval camp of biblical terrors, primitive suspicions, a
choice must be made by all lovers of peace: either to bring it
into the modern world, into a rational state of being within
that spirit of human partnership, a capacity for which has been
so amply demonstrated by every liberated black nation on our
continent, or—to bring it abjectly to its knees by ejecting it, in

every aspect, from humane recognition, so that it caves in internally, through the strategies of its embattled majority. Whatever the choice, this inhuman affront cannot be allowed to pursue our twentieth century conscience into the twenty-first, that symbolic coming-of-age which peoples of all cultures appear to celebrate with rites of passage. That calendar, we know, is not universal, but time is, and so are the imperatives of time. And of those imperatives that challenge our being, our presence, and humane definition at this time, none can be considered more pervasive than the end of racism, the eradication of human inequality, and the dismantling of all their structures.

# 5 *Reading And Writing*

# *The Human Dilemma*

ROLLO MAY

*Dr. May is
internationlly recognized for his outstanding contributions to psychology. He has received Phi Beta Kappa's
Ralph Waldo Emerson Award for humane scholarship,
The Christopher Award for affirming the highest values
of the human spirit, The American Psychological
Association's Award for Distinguished Contribution to
the Science and Profession of Clinical Psychology and its
Gold Medal Award for a Distinguished Career. Dr. May
is author of more than 25 books, all still in print. His*
**Love and Will** *and* **Courage to Create** *were
bestsellers. Also he has written* **My Quest for Beauty**
*and* **Paulus, Tillich as Spiritual Teacher.** *His
current book is* **The Cry for Myth.**

Once in a while I catch myself having a curious fantasy. It goes something like this.

A writer arrives at the heavenly gates at the end of his long and productive life. He is brought up before St. Peter for his customary accounting. Formidable, St. Peter sits calmly behind his table looking like the Moses of Michelangelo. An angel assistant in a white jacket drops a manila folder on the table which St. Peter opens and looks at, frowning. Despite the awesome visage of the judge, the writer clutches his briefcase and steps up with commendable courage.

But St. Peter's frown deepens; he drums with his fingers on the table and grunts a few nondirective "uhm-uhm"s as he fixes the candidate with his Mosaic eyes.

The silence is discomfiting. Finally the writer opens his briefcase and cries, "Here! The reprints of my hundred and thirty-two books."

St. Peter slowly shakes his head.

Burrowing deeper into the briefcase the writer offers, "Let me submit the awards I received for my writing." St. Peter's frown is unabated as he silently continues to stare into the writer's face and his tone is like Moses breaking the news of the ten commandments: "You are charged with *nimis simplicando*! oversimplifying!" You have spent your life making molehills out of mountains, that's what you're guilty of. When man was tragic, you made him trivial. When he was picaresque, you called him picayune. When he suffered passively, you described him as simpering; and when he drummed up enough courage to act, you made him a non-hero. Man had passion; you called it 'satisfaction,' and when you were relaxed and looking at your secretary you called it 'release of tension.' You made man over into the image of your childhood Erector Set.

The writer steps back. "Your honor, I only tried to let man speak for himself!"

St. Peter levels a long bony finger at the writer. "You thought everybody could be fooled. Everybody but you. You always assumed that you, the fooler, were never fooled! Not very consistent, is it?"

St. Peter sighs. The writer opens his mouth, but St. Peter raises his hand. "Please! Not your well-practiced chatter. Something new is required . . . something new." He sits back, meditating . . .

And about that time I find myself meditating too.

What is the human dilemma?

It has to do with subjective inner reality and objective information about what is outside. In other words, *the human dilemma is that which arises out of a man's capacity to experience himself as both subject and object at the same time.*

Now to sharpen our definition: We are not simply describing two alternate ways of behaving. Nor is it quite accurate to speak of our being subject and object *simultaneously.* The important point is that our consciousness is a process of oscillation between the two. Writing in any genuine sense lies not in the capacity to live as "pure subject," but rather in the capacity to experience *both* modes, to live in the dialectical relationship.

Since a number of authors, including myself, have endeavored elsewhere to describe this capacity in greater detail, I shall not go into its infinitely wide implications here. I shall only add that we readers have the same human dilemma as we authors.

We have assiduously avoided confronting this human dilemma. Out of our seemingly omnipresent reductive tendency, we omit aspects of human functioning which are essential. And we end up without the "inner person to whom these things happen." We are left with only the "things of information" that happen, suspended in mid-air.

We need to confront, for one example, the *historical dimension* of ourselves and the human beings we read about, as well as the history of the culture in which we live and move and have our being. It is a failure to see things in their historical dimension which have made us blind to the dangers in our phenomenal growth.

We need, furthermore, to confront *literature*, especially classical literature. For the classics are that because they have expressed some unchanging aspects of human experience, ministering to human beings when they were written and to different ages and cultures ever since. Literature is the self-interpretation of human beings throughout history.

Literature carries two other concerns that we need to confront; namely, the perdurable *symbols* and *myths*. These communicate, in ways that bridge different ages and cultures, the essence of what it has meant and means to be human. Symbols and myths are the nonmaterial structure which is the basis for our culture, and it is the symbols and myths that are ailing in a disruptive time like our own. They speak directly out of the human dilemma. How can we minister to the ailments of human beings if we are strangers to their deepest language?

But if we confront the human dilemma, we shall at least then be dealing with human beings rather than with some absurd and truncated creatures reduced to isolated parts of information with no center whatever, parts that we can read about since they fit our information machines. It will mean giving up some of our own power needs and clarifying our needs to control. We can then have some hope that we may endure.

# The Art of Writing Novels

## JOANNE LEEDOM-ACKERMAN

*Joanne Leedom-Ackerman,
an award-winning journalist, won immediate acclaim
with the publication of her short story collection, **No
Marble Angels**. Her current book is the bestselling
novel, **The Dark Path to the River**.*

When I was younger, I held slabs of ice together with my bare feet as Eliza leapt to freedom in Harriet Beecher Stowe's *Uncle Tom's Cabin* I went underground for a time and lived in a room with a thousand light bulbs, along with Ralph Ellison's *Invisible Man*. And I was in the corner of the barn watching with awe as Rose of Sharon bared her breast and nursed a starving man in John Steinbeck's *Grapes of Wrath*.

The power of the imagination to take an author's images, scenes, and characters and to bind them to one's own life, to draw from them wisdom *and* experience, makes the reading of a novel an intimate act which television, movies, and even plays can't equal. The novel's unique power comes in part from the personal nature of both its creation and reception. A novel is the product of one writer, working alone in a room, distilling experience, history and myth through his or her imagination and turning out a story. The reader is also alone, interacting from the basis of personal history.

For every novel written, there are different stories of its genesis and gestation. However, there are also some generalities which I think will hold, for novelists from wide-ranging backgrounds and time periods and working habits seem to have found common ground.

One generalization is that the novel creates the writer as much as the writer creates the novel. The novelist studies writing technique by reading and writing constantly. But the best novels are products of vision and sensibility as well as narrative technique.

In an essay in his book *Shadow and Act*, Ralph Ellison notes,

. . . as I continued, I made a most perplexing discovery; namely, that for all his conscious concern with technique, a writer did not so much create the novel as he was created by the novel. That is, one did not make an arbitrary gesture when one sought to write. And when I say that the novelist is created by the novel, I mean to remind

you that fictional techniques are not a mere set of objective tools, but something much more intimate: a way of
feeling and seeing and of expressing one's sense of life.
And the process of *acquiring* technique is a process of
modifying one's responses, of learning to see and feel, to
hear and observe, to evoke and evaluate the images of
memory and of summoning up and directing the imagination; of learning to conceive of human values in the
ways which have been established by the great writers
who have developed and extended the art. And perhaps
the writer's greatest freedom, as artist, lies precisely in his
possession of technique; for it is through technique that
he comes to possess and express the meaning of this life.

Thus viewed, technique for the novelist begins with how
he sees life. The writing of a novel demands a certain truth-
telling. It is not an act of will so much as an act of listening.
Learning to listen to the characters and story is part of learning
technique.

Harriet Beecher Stowe felt she was possessed by her
story. Over the years she had witnessed or read about the
events of slavery. She had read a newspaper account of a
young slave woman fleeing over the icy Ohio River with her
child. Stowe herself had had a black child whom she taught in
a school in her home be suddenly seized from his mother and
taken back to Kentucky and put up for auction. She had lis-
tened and watched, but it wasn't until she felt impelled to
begin writing that her characters and story took her over.
When her publisher suggested that she must keep her book
shorter because she was writing on an unpopular subject
which might be hard to sell, she replied that she did not make
the story, that the story made itself, and that she could not stop
until it was done.

Stowe, Ellison, and Steinbeck all took on the politics of
their times. They used individual experience to create
archetypes in character and develop stories which became

myths of American life. Politics by its nature is a group activity, the expression of the group's will, but fiction in its essence is individual, rooted in character and emotion. Learning the difference is also an essential part of mastering the techniques of fiction.

The writer learns, Ellison has noted, "that he is involved with values which turn in their own way, and not in the way of politics, upon the central issues affecting his nation and his time."

Ellison, Steinbeck and Stowe are among the writers I've turned to in studying both technique and values. I hesitate to insert personal experience in the company of such writers, but I presume to do so because they have been my teachers.

Growing up in the South in the 1950s and 60s, I spent much of my early years debating issues of civil rights with family and friends. For a long time I located the antagonist outside myself, in politics, society and culture; thus I could separate myself from it. I became a journalist, and as a reporter in the East, I gathered facts and statistics and social opinions and searched for answers to issues. But all the while other stories were building in me which couldn't so easily be contained in facts and figures and social theory. I didn't call these stories a novel because I didn't know how they would end. But I knew the face of the emotion I wanted to address and the face of a character or two. I also knew two sentences. The first: "The girl did not belong." The second: "There are no marble angels in potter's field." That first sentence is the opening of "The Tutor," one of the stories in the short story collection *No Marble Angels*. The second sentence didn't survive, at least not in that form though its remnant is in the title story.

Let me quote from the opening scene of "The Tutor":

The girl did not belong. It was obvious to those watching her walk up Shenandoah Avenue. Under her arm she carried a notebook and a shopping bag. She moved slowly down the street, her eyes darting from side to side, large, curious eyes peering out from under her bangs, observing the squat brick houses, the people on their stoops. Those watching thought perhaps she was a welfare worker making her rounds. Every few steps she glanced into her notebook then again scanned the porches. She smiled, a shy, tentative smile which asked these strangers to smile back at her. It was her smile, her peculiar bidding, which hinted to the neighbors she was not from welfare.

Others watching guessed she was a walker, out soliciting business. Tight jeans, loose shirt. "Hot tonight, baby, right hot." One of the locals clucked as he sidled up beside her. She glanced at the pavement and walked faster. Hips set high, a little wide, legs long and slim, breasts small under the cotton shirt. She dodged these men like the hockey player she'd been in college, not like a jane on the make. "Hey, green jeans, where you going?" the men called. She flashed a cautious, not-to-be-rude smile then hurried down the block without looking back. On the porches the women, on the streets the men, watched this white girl passing.

At No. 14 Shenandoah, the girl stopped. She shut her notebook and climbed the broken steps to the porch. She ran her hand around the waist of her slacks, tucking in her shirt; then she brushed fingers through her short dark hair. She started towards the front door but stopped. The house looked empty. The shades were drawn, the windows patched with the *Afro American*. The window frames, swollen past their shape, had been stuffed with rags, and she could see no light inside. On the rotten post which propped up the porch she read a message scrawled in red, "Fuck Them Zoro Lives!", scrawled anonymously then covered over and over with paint by whoever lived there, painted over and over again.

She finally moved to the door and knocked.

Silence.

She knocked again.

From between a chain lock, a face peered out.

"Who you?"

"I'm . . . I'm the tutor." She disliked that word. "I'm Shannon Douglass, is your mother home?"

"Ma-a-a-!" the voice shouted down the hall. "That tutor lady's here."

The door shut, then opened. She had begun.

So I began a journey of my own by considering experience from the inside out. With that scene I began my first novel, and gradually my writing and direction changed, from the journalistic consideration of the body politic, culture, society, to the consideration of the individual heart, from the objective to the subjective. With this change grew a conviction that the individual, heeded through art, could illumine a whole.

It seems to me now that this illumination comes at the point when one's experience and imagination intersect and take flight. By experience I don't necessarily mean the day-to-day events of one's life, but one's emotional knowledge. As a writer or as anyone who is able to take that knowledge and extend it and apply it both to himself and outside of himself, he is able to encompass larger worlds while at the same time closing the distance between the self and the other until that distance often fades and instead becomes the shadow of one's own face.

Writers are often asked: did that really happen? Is that just you you're writing about, disguising yourself as tall and thin and calling yourself Sue? I've never yet heard a writer give a direct answer to that question, I'm sure because however close one may start to one's own experience, something else happens in the process. Characters have minds of their own. They tell you: that may be your life, but this is mine so sit back and listen. If you're smart, you do; and a larger life experience begins to take over. As the writer listens to his characters and to their story, he takes down the world the way they see it, shaping it according to their experience, which is never quite the same as his own.

I don't mean to mystify the process, but after a novelist has studied his craft, studied the tools of narrative, scenes, dialogue, monologues, exposition, after he has studied the subject he's writing about, after he has sharpened his pencils, he is then left alone in a room with a sheet of paper and himself. As he listens, his characters will begin to offer him clues of the story he is to tell: a coin, a flower, a gesture, a word. If the writer doesn't rush them or force them, the characters will unfold their story, much of which the writer may already know, and yet the characters always know more than he and will reveal it only in the process of the writing.

I'd like to end with part of a letter from John Steinbeck to his editor Pascal Covici during the writing of *East of Eden*

> ... this book is growing so fast that I can't keep up with it. I don't know what I am going to do. I told you that every part of it had pups. That's the trouble. And here is another thing that is almost frightening, the story comes to me as though I were reading it but not in its final form. Then I must take the story I have heard in my ears and set it down. It is a very curious thing and one that is driving me.

# Wordsmithing

JAMES F. T. BUGENTAL

*Dr. Bugental is
visiting distinguished Professor at the California School
of Professional Psychology, Emeritus Professor of the
Saybrook Institute, and a diplomate in clinical
psychology from the American Board of Professional
Psychology. He has served as president of the
Association of Humanistic Psychology and was the
recipient of the 1988 Rollo May award for contributions
to the literary pursuit. His many books include*
**The Search for Existential Identity and
Intimate Journeys,** *to be published in 1990.*

He hated his life. He hated life. It was all—his favorite word—shit. "I don't know why the fuck I'm here to waste your time and mine . . . and my money . . . must be nuts to come to a shrink. Anyway, what can you, or anyone, do for me?"

It wasn't a question; it was a denial and just a little bit of a challenge. That little bit was all the hope he could muster.

Frank, a bellman in a cheap hotel, had little reason, indeed, to love life or to hope for himself. A shattered family in his past, a dull dead-end job in his present, and if he continued the petty thefts he was beginning to make habitual, a prison cell in his future. He knew Sartre's question, why not suicide?

He knew Sartre's question!

Frank read. Frank read constantly. His friends were books. His dreams were from books. His hope was in books. He came to psychotherapy because of books, and ultimately he was supported through the pain, discouragement, and demands of therapy by books.

Eventually Frank changed his life, went back to school, took an advanced degree, even began to try to write books himself. As his second therapist, I feel good about our work together, but I know I never would have seen Frank nor would I have been able to help him had he not been a reader above anything else. Books were his first therapist.

I am a psychotherapist and author, and I offer these thoughts about the wordsmith's craft and its broader setting in our lives from that perspective. I chose "wordsmith" for my title because I believe that our art is inexorably changing, but that the craft of forging words into something more than words is now central in human life and will become even more so.

We are each of us at once separate from all other humans and yet related to all others. This is fundamental to human nature, and it is within this paradox that the wordsmith's craft is set.

Beginning to put words onto the screen or on paper is venturing out into a large sea in a rather small boat. While I may have plotted my course, I can never be certain that I will

end up in the port chosen at the outset. Writing promises
adventure, discovery, disappointment, confusion, and an impe-
tus to personal change. Even the simplest letter to a friend can
unexpectedly bring into view islands not on my charts or sea
monsters to disrupt my confident passage.

What is this sea? It is the depths of subjective possibility,
the always encompassing range of the unknown within myself,
the beyond-the-horizon mystery that we often conspire to
ignore but that is, nevertheless, continually present and subtly
influencing what we experience. Our subjectivity is the realm
of our thoughts and feelings, of dreaming and creativity, of
love and hate, of aspiration and dread. Subjectivity is the well
from which wordsmiths draw their raw material and it is the
goal toward which they direct their efforts.

The wordsmith's craft is set in the space between persons.
This is, in a very real sense, a space between worlds, the
worlds of our individual subjectivities. The miracle is that we
can in some way communicate across that unfathomable gap,
although we can never really cross it.

Much of the freight carried by the words that voyage
across inter-person space arises from the subjectivity of one
person and is intended to produce a subjective event in the
other person or persons. It is primarily a process of trying to
call into being an *experience* in that other person, although the
longer term intent may be to move that other person to do or
not do or say something.

"Intersubjective evocation" is a way of naming the process by which one person produces from his/her own subjectivity (intention, knowledge, artistry), words and other media
with the purpose of causing another person to have a certain
kind of subjective experience. The passages above about Frank,
the bellman, and that below, which contrast my loving feelings
and my sense of horror, seek to evoke in the reader's subjectivity experiences comparable to those I know within myself.

The next three paragraphs are quoted from *The Search for
Existential Identity* (Jossey-Bass, 1976).

Deep in the night she stirs in my embrace, and I dimly awaken. My arm is numb from her loved weight. Gently, quietly, I try to pull it free, reluctantly parting from her warmth. She turns, still sleeping, murmurs my name and some vague syllables, loving sounds. I try to make out the precious words, but they slide into the abyss of her sleep. Suddenly that seems terribly, unredeemably tragic. Now wide awake, I know I am overreacting, but at the same moment I want to cry out, to stop time, to know the now forever-lost reaching of her soul toward mine. How can we two, who have come through so much together, be so separate that I will never know those words?

Another night, another place, and I am reading the searching words of Allen Wheelis as he examines our human guilt. He is recalling the horror of the Dacca racetrack when four suspected Pakastani quislings were tortured to death before 5,000 cheering Bengalis. I am sickened. I don't want to remember what I pushed out of my thoughts when I first read of it in Time several years ago. And then the secret, the obscene, the persistent thoughts come: Did they do this to them? and that? My God! I don't want to think about it. How could I sit in those stands and watch? Could I have been one of the torturers? I don't want to know, but I do: I could have been in those bleachers screaming for the blood. I could have been down on the field, imagining more terrible ways to extract the last bit of anguish. I am brother to the torturer, the killer.

And I could have been one of those tied to the stakes, helplessly awaiting the next terrible inspiration. I know that kinship as well.

Wordsmiths (authors, editors, publishers), depth psychotherapists, spiritual teachers, and artists of all kinds are among the chief professionals working in the inter-person space, using words and their auxiliaries (gestures, facial expression, intonations, etc.) to effect desired intersubjective evocations.

Still there are the times when words serve our solitude as well: When one engages in the work or play of thinking alone, writing serves to carry a monologue forward into a kind of reflexive dialogue. For many of us that is one of the joys of solitary activity and of writing.

Note: In the following paragraphs, by way of giving further point, I will speak bluntly and from my own value system. I do not pretend to be objective in this matter, and I do not believe it would be either possible or desirable. I know others have quite contrasting views on these matters; but the interactive process between persons is best forwarded when we each say our own truths while striving to be open to hear others also. One other note, in what follows, I employ the concept of addiction. I mean it literally, not as simile.

The greatest present danger to our world is addiction, and the drug of greatest threat is power. Addiction to power is subtle in its early stages, but again and again it destroys. As Lord Acton wisely wrote, "Power tends to corrupt, and absolute power corrupts absolutely."

This truth is acted out in all walks of life: in the political arena (e.g., Reagan, Mussolini), the religious (the renaissance popes, Jim Jones), industrial leaders (Henry Ford), and among artists, educators, critics, and all fields where power accumulates in individuals.

Most power-addicts show a similar pattern of starting out humane and broad in vision, then achieving increased power, and, as that occurs, becoming blind to their earlier values and acting out their drug-induced dreams of supreme righteousness. This is, of course, the essence of tragedy, the hubris which leads to the downfall of the once great hero.

It is important to recognize that this pattern involves a movement from an early recognition of subjective kinship and thus an unusual ability to speak to the subjective yearnings of their followers. Then, as the power-drug takes hold, the addict loses the sense of perspective and the awareness of his or her followers as having subjective centers of their own. Now the followers become objects to be moved to satisfy the increasing doses of power required by the addict.

The significance of all this for our concerns in this essay is this: With the further development of the wordsmith's craft, it will be more than ever called to the service of those who want to control the minds and lives of others. Two examples suffice: Leni Riefenstahl served Hitler's addiction; a succession of public relations people has covered for Reagan's confusions, distortions, and denials. The moral is as obvious as it is frightening: The democratic dream is likely to die in the death grip of money and the wordsmith's art.

Yet there is hope. By and large wordsmiths tend to be those who believe in the value of the human. This is not a fortunate chance; it is in the very nature of those who serve the subjective that they come to believe in and cherish the mystery which is at the heart of each person. They write to reach and stimulate that mystery, and out of that mystery come wonders.

A melodramatic word? Perhaps, but if wonders exist, they take forms which range from the common place to the truly miraculous. An 80-year-old woman writes her first book and it becomes a bestseller. The granddaughter of slaves becomes a superb stylist. A Vietnam veteran lets a locomotive cut his legs off to make a statement about his hatred of war. A sad, angry, hotel bellman gradually relinquishes most of his rage, subjects himself to the inanities and avails himself of the opportunities of graduate education, and becomes a contributor rather than a drain on his world.

So long as our media are free, we who practice the craft of wordsmithing can and must sound the alarm, try to bring our art to the awakening of the human spirit, the freeing of human intention, and the preserving of our future as truly ours.

# *Writing in the Human Sciences*

RICHARD YOUNG

*Dr. Richard Young is
a practicing psyschotherapist and head of the Psychology
Department at California Baptist College. He has
written and lectured extensively in the area of human
behavior and is currently writing a collection of stories,
thoughts, and reflections entitled, **Confessions of a
Prodigal: Letters from a Far Country.***

A little boy sat nervously on the large front steps of his house waiting for his dad to come home from work. It was twilight and a chilly October breeze was blowing fallen leaves across the yard. The old stone steps radiated the cold through his denim trousers and made him wish that he was inside standing over the gas floor furnace in the hall. But he had to wait. He sat with his pudgy, pinchable cheeks resting in his small hands and stared at the street corner where his dad's big blue car appeared every evening about this time. Why did his little sister always have to come in his room and bother his stuff? Sometimes he wished that he didn't even have a little sister. Why did she have to be such a brat? He hadn't really hit her that hard, but she went crying to mom anyway. What a baby. If she could have just left his room when he told her to, he wouldn't be sitting here right now waiting to tell his dad what he had done. It wasn't fair.

He saw a flash of blue out of the corner of his eye as the car turned onto their street. For a brief moment it was painted yellow by the glow of the huge amber streetlight that he always liked to swing on when they all walked to the store for ice cream on Saturday afternoons. As the big car pulled slowly into the driveway, he saw his dad wave and smile, but the tightness in his chest and throat kept him from waving back. He watched his father lock the car and move towards him in giant strides across the leaf-clustered yard.

"What's the matter, pal?" his father said, as he bent down so that he could see into his son's pale green eyes.

At first the words fairly raced out of the little boy's mouth. "Lisa came into my room without permission, and she almost broke my model airplane that you gave me for Christmas, and I tried to make her leave and she wouldn't, so I hit her and now mom's mad at me and . . ." He stopped suddenly, almost as much for being out of words as for seeing the smile slowly fade from his father's face. In that moment, it almost seemed as if the anger he had so carefully nurtured towards his sister for the past years just disappeared as the first tears began to make their long journey towards his chin.

His father looked steadily into his eyes and said, "I don't care what happened. It's never okay to hit. It's never okay. Do you understand?"

"Yes daddy, I know, but Lisa . . . "

"No buts. It's never okay."

"I know, I'm really sorry."

His father picked him up in his strong arms and held him close as he walked up the steps towards the front door. "I know that it's not always easy being the big brother. But you do it pretty good most of the time."

As they passed through the front door into the warmth of the living room, the little boy buried his face in his father's neck. And he felt big.


This is a simple little story about a simple, important moment in the life of a child. As a psychotherapist, I could explain in great detail the ideas about parent-child relationships that moved me to write this story. But then the story would lose some of its magic and the ideas would lose their power. Most importantly, you might miss the opportunity to interpret it in the context of your own experience and for the child within you to discover the truths it attempts to communicate through reading.

Milton Erickson, the famous hypnotherapist, believed that the greatest teachings are those that reach down into the unconscious mind. Such "unconscious learnings" involve an intuitive understanding of symbolic meanings and universal-individual truths and are less concerned with rational thoughts, ideas, and facts. When we are moved or inspired by an experience, it is because our unconscious has been touched and changed. Erickson also believed that these learnings occur more easily in the natural kind of trance states that we experience when we allow ourselves to be carried away by reading the words of an author or by a work of art, or a piece of music. At such moments, we surrender ourselves to the experience and are briefly transported inward to a place of timelessness, wisdom, and wholeness. We learn best when we are entranced.

Those of us who write, especially those of us who write nonfiction, attempt to share information in a way that will educate, engage, and perhaps even inspire the reader. We try to communicate the truth, however we may see it, in the sincere belief that the truth will ultimately set us free. But in our earnest attempt to be clear and precise, rational and accurate, we often forget how to speak to the human heart. In the name of scientific objectivity, we drain all the passion from our words and render our message sterile and powerless. By aiming only at the head, we miss the soul.

*The power of story.* All of the great moral teachers and social innovators of history have been master storytellers. Buddha and Christ, Gandhi and Martin Luther King all liked to tell a good story. These were men who knew how to speak in a way that could change a person's heart and mind. There is something almost magical about stories of real people facing real dilemmas as well as parables of imaginary people and events that put us in touch with ourselves and others. Somehow they enable us to integrate previously unknown or disparate parts of our personalities into a greater unity and to experience our connectedness to other human beings. Besides all that, they make us feel good.

Facts are all well and good but they are easily forgotten while stories, and the truths they contain, are not. Do you remember your phone number when you were five years old? Probably you don't, but how about the story of Cinderella or the Prodigal Son? After having created them internally, usually through reading, they become a living part of you. Erickson once said that if you want to learn how to become a good therapist or a good teacher, start telling stories to eight-year-olds. I think he would have offered the same advice to writers.

*The power of humor.* Norman Cousins has taught us all a very important lesson about the healing power of laughter. And researchers are finding that people who laugh frequently live longer than those who don't. In the olden days, various religious groups thought that frivolity was a sin. Laughter was an opportunity for the Devil to have his way with us. While humor is no longer considered a sin (except by college professors), there are rumors circulating in some quarters that it is unscientific. No joke.

Writers who can make us laugh at our own foolishness and the foolishness of others present us with a very special gift of life. One of the most satisfying books that I have read in recent months is a small collection of science essays entitled *Natural Acts*, by David Quammen. This author seems to accept the heretical notion that scientific facts have a greater half-life in the human cortex when they are presented humorously. I find myself frequently going back to this slim volume of solid science to read once more why he considers mosquitoes to be nature's Viet Cong and why octopi suffer from mental disorders. Somebody, please, teach us to laugh again.

*The power of conviction.* Man is a symbolic creature, a creator of symbolic universes through language and reading. It is this very fact that enables us to search for symbolic meaning in all areas of our experience and, in fact, compels us to do so. This capacity is the genesis of human values and personality. In plain language, we are believers. It is not enough for us to objectively know; we must also subjectively believe.

It is redundant but nonetheless true to state that we live in an age of information. Those of us who have taken it upon ourselves to share that information in written form have become too objective. We are taught to present the facts dispassionately and let the reader decide for himself. We desperately avoid imposing our values on others or alienating those who might believe differently from the way we do, all in the interest of intellectual rigor. As a result, we write too much with too little conviction and rob our words of their power to make a lasting impact on the lives of those who read our work. We need to take more chances. We need to find the courage to write what we believe and believe what we write. Not everyone is going to like it. We will be accused by some of being irrational, subjective or dogmatic. We will be told by others that we made a difference, and isn't that the point?

People have a unique ability to listen for the truth and to allow themselves to be moved and inspired by it. As writers, we can help them in this process by employing techniques that entrance, enchant, and fascinate the reader. We can present the facts humorously, we can use examples, stories, and parables, and we can communicate passionately with conviction. We can make people feel big.

# 6 Reading And Education

# *The Humanities*

RICHARD W. WISEMAN

*Dr. Wiseman*
*is a professor of the humanities at San Francisco*
*State University. He is the author of*
*numerous scholarly articles.*

In the 60s and early 70s, when the demand for "relevant" education was made, many or most faculties of the universities of America capitulated.

Progressive courses were quickly sketched; experiential learning and absolute democracy. In the new classrooms all sat in a circle and made equal, utterly equal contributions to the procedure and the process. Other cultures invaded, Zen and Castaneda as well as Hermann Hesse as well as *The Catcher in the Rye*. They were worshipped as the new possibilities, the voices of the new times.

In terms of values for the 80s and values for the next century, it seemed relatively easy to convict the old-fashioned standards and classics of inadequacy. How could tenacious study of Virgil, Plato, Dante, even Shakespeare and Montaigne prepare bright, young citizens for the coming of terrorism, disaster in earth's ecology, starvation and overpopulation, new attitudes toward euthanasia, lifestyles, women's new position and the militant women's liberation movement, sexual prefer-ences, and the like?

But, alas, the new materials of relevant information were particularly incapable of giving direction, purpose, incentive, conviction, and hope. Just as the old modalities had failed, so too the new ones were failing.

A digression to the Jungian perspective insists upon inclusion here. In Erich Neumann's *Art and the Creative Uncon-scious* there is a splendid diagram: It is a picture of the old, guiding, centering energies of religion and of all manifestations of our culture as it used to be, showing how they are disinte-grating on every hand, a shopworn, tiresome theme, but clear-ly linked to the brute fact that the new images and energies that will persuade us where we must now go, how we must now live, are not visible over the horizon of time. We could juxtapose this cultural image with the educational images we have been discussing. Those Platonic "permanent questions" like the power of Christian doctrine, seem to have lost their chance to stimulate and enthrall; for years they have only been vapid repetitions of our greatness, a greatness that used to be possible.

So, this leaves us with the dilemma of process. We must abide the question of values, it seems; much more pain and labor must be expended, much shaping must take place, before we have materials that rival the scope and profundity of our great tradition. But, if we assume for a moment that any rigorous training sharpens the ability of the human mind and spirit, just as any leather strap will hone the razor, then do we not have a usefulness in our classes that we have lost sight of? The classics were not written in stone, for indeed, we recall, Moses even broke those original stone tablets of the law. But like the tables of the law, the stone tablets of our tradition did provide an unprecedented body of material that could compel us to winnow and sort our own life challenges, our decisions, with unusual acuity.

Any absolute values inculcated from books can be useful only in a general way, aspects of human character and human loving. But to make those students adequate to the new world, what else can be done for them except to mold, sharpen, and enrich their minds and personalities by compelling them to come again and again to the barricade of thought and insight, by seeing to it that they, again and again, penetrate to this core meaning and prepare themselves to stand before a vast body of confusing information while heading toward the heart of the matter.

It is clear that this premise shifts the entire argument about the closing of the American mind; and considered *sub specie aeternitatis*, those arguments about education must often turn on just such a new premise. Let me repeat and exaggerate for the sake of emphasis. We have no pathway as yet in the arena of values. If we place many of the new materials beside the conservative, old classical works we can see at a glance which area is more demanding and which will force the process of change I have been discussing above.

A question that has emerged in recent years and which cannot find any direct help from the great tradition of our culture is that of nature conservancy, the protection of the earth planet itself from the threat of extinction. This threat comes from unheard of new situations such as drastic overpopulation, nuclear energy, and brutally changing attitudes in many parts of the world.

The question we are constantly asking might be phrased thus: How can education set things up so that most of the students will want to do all the things that education wants them to do? So that they will see the only meaning in their lives in doing them? Inevitably one thinks here of the ironic method of much of modern literature. The great modern author or poet frequently has a specific attitude in mind but pretends to espouse a very different way. By dint of his hidden persuasions, the reader can come to a point where he obstinately takes a stand exactly where the author hoped he would take a stand. Can we do this with modern education?

I want to try now to address a pathway to values which might develop from computers, word processors, machines, modern technology invading the schools of America from preschool upward. We need the necessary critical force to see what is taking place in all of this.

Instead of addressing the works of Minsky or Roszak or Sherry Turkell or even Shabahangi, I want to pursue this entire problem on the basis of a fictional statement. In the very recent work by Ursula LeGuin called *Always Coming Home*, the author gives us her perception of the proper role of computers and high technology and artificial intelligence in a balanced world to come. The novel is presumably a vision of a much simpler society in the Napa valley in northern California, perhaps some 500 or 600 years in the future. The people in this novel live much closer to their traditions, their histories, much closer to their land and their loves, their homes. In addition to the warm and loving life in the many villages of the region, there is a group of cities with a special function. Indeed, there are two kinds of cities. One is called the city of mind. In order to make clear what Ursula LeGuin is proposing, I shall need to quote from page 156 of her novel:

> The business of the city of mind was, apparently, the business of any species or individual: to go on existing. Its existence consisted essentially in information. Its observable activity was entirely related to the collection, storage, and collation of data, including the historical records of cybernetic and human populations back as far as material was available from documentary or archaeological evidence; description and history of all life forms on the planet, ancient and current, physical description of the material world on all levels from the subatomic through the chemical . . .

We need not carry this further to see what these cities of mind could accomplish. One extremely interesting statement has to do with the fact that these isolated computerized cities are there only to serve the populations who have need for a certain kind of information. The author explains: "Information went both ways through the exchanges; the nature and quantity of the information was up to the human end of the partnership. The city did not issue unrequested information. It sometimes requested, never demanded information."

We have only to ponder the gentle suggestiveness of these last sentences to see what Ursula LeGuin has been asking us to think about. In her vision of a truly livable future world, the usefulness of highly technical scientific machines is not denied, however; their only point and function has to do with requests for information. If no request for information is issued, then no information is forthcoming.

Now the interesting question emerges, can this type of imaginative projection stimulate the young people who are now growing up blindly capable of using computers and calculators and high-tech machinery, but who are blindly incapable of drawing back from that information and seeing its usefulness? Can they then be changed by reading novels such as the one we have been looking at, so that they will have a different concept of machine and of life?

# The Electronic Revolution

*Frederick Turner is
Founders Professor of Arts and Humanities at the
University of Texas at Dallas and is the former editor of
the Kenyon Review. He is a regular contributor to
Harper's Magazine and is the author of a novel,
A Double Shadow, and books of criticism including
Shakespeare and the Nature of Time and Natural
Classicism. His books of poetry include The Garden
and The New World. Genesis, an epic poem, was
published in the fall of 1988.*

What do human beings do when they encounter a task too great for their powers? They use tools, prostheses to bridge over the regions of weakness and thus connect and enable the regions of strength. Such tools are more various in their nature than we sometimes imagine. They include those prosthetic enzymes, the ferments, yeasts, and molds by which we eke out the weaknesses of our digestive systems and to which we owe our bread, our cheese, our wine; also the rules of our art-forms, such as counterpoint, perspective, meter, by which we amplify and extend the integrative powers of our minds; and of course those more familiar tools, like automobiles, violins, communications satellites, garden hoses, and hiking boots, by which we assist our muscles.

For centuries the most potent tool that humanity has possessed has been books; and indeed a book with an index and a margin for notes is a formidably compact, cheap, and powerful tool of great elegance and simplicity, and in many ways superbly adapted to the human brain and body. But printed books were themselves the answer to a crisis in information-processing, a crisis that historians call the rise of the middle class. They were invented as prostheses to supplement the marvelous but finally inadequate information-processing system of the Middle Ages, which combined script and icon with various psychic technologies, such as narrative, meter, rhetoric, drama, the disputation, and the associative memory systems.

Today the sheer numbers of books, their uncorrectability, and their linear, stereotyped, and deterministic form, have in turn rendered them incapable of handling on their own the integrative demands of the enormous information flow that they themselves helped to create. A new tool offers itself to the academy: the computer. Can it help?

Before we go any further, it is vital to point out that new information-processing tools do not necessarily extinguish old ones. The fundamental psychic technologies—story, meter, musical tonality, and so on can never be rendered obsolete, as they are the most effective channels of communication or interfaces with the human brain. Though the "memory-theater" of the medieval and renaissance mnemonic systems was effectively replaced by print, most of the other information-processing systems are still very much alive, and may even be stronger than ever if we take into account the much larger proportion of the population that has access to them. It is significant that the greatest drama of all, that of William Shakespeare, was composed at the very moment of the triumph of the printed book; for drama is an ancient oral-audial psychic technology, essentially independent of print. By the same token, we might well expect that the greatest glory of the book as a work of art still lies in the future, once the electronic media and the computer have taken from it the baser burdens it must bear today.

So we must see the computer as in partnership with, even amplifying, the older information technologies. What can it bring to the partnership?

First, of course, the compact storage and easy retrievability of huge databases. With compact-disk storage the computer now far surpasses the book in this respect; and the book was until now the most efficient information storage and retrieval device. More important, a computer database is not limited to a single index, but can construct a new index entry to the precise requirements of the reader in a fraction of a second. Related to this feature are the infinite correctability of computer data and the infinitely wide "margin" for notes and comments that it offers. Books are much more limited in this respect; computer text is live text, like the lyrics of a folk ballad or oral epic. The fixity of book text requires a sharp division between the easy creative flow and messy approximateness of the rehearsal, the sketch, the rough draft on one hand, and the lifeless finality of the finished version on the other. In the computer this division vanishes; each new version is the final version.

The computer can organize information as it is organized in the real world, that is, in a dynamic, branched, multi-dimensional hierarchy. In this respect, computer information is more like pictorial than printed information but without the limitation to two dimensions (plus one for the "stretched" picture, in perspective). Music, discourse, oratory and book text are all forced to spin out their information into a single one-dimensional linear thread. Thus computer text echoes in its shape and format the new hierarchical form of the universe as it comes clearly into view.

One consequence of this last feature is that computer information is, so to speak, free. At each of the branch points of the information tree there is a choice, and the correctability of computer text (together with its formidable capacity to read just the whole system to one change, as in the spreadsheet or word processor index function) makes it possible to originate new branch points and new branches anywhere.

Given this "branchiness," computer information can closely model the interdisciplinary nature of the real world. It is not disorganized, as book text tends to be, by digression; and what is digression but the very principle of order, subordination, control and freedom in real physical systems? Each branch of a tree is a fertile digression. A book must stick to its subject, and therefore carefully fenced off "subject areas" must be defined. A computer program can store under any entry a whole world of subordinate information, which may belong to another discipline altogether in the old dispensation. The footnote is but a clumsy approximation to this ability.

"Branchiness" in turn makes possible the *interactive* character of computer information. The reader is always also a writer, a participant observer. Now in this respect the computer mode takes a great leap backwards, to the interactiveness of oral modes of information processing, without losing the accuracy, stability, and immortality of book text.

The interactiveness of computer information fosters a closer bond between the text and the endorphin and catecholamine reward system of the human brain. The brain rewards itself for a completed cycle of action and feedback. Literature, poetry, stories, etc.—is a way of making book text interactive so as to activate this reward system, but it takes genius to fold most types of information down into such springy forms as will maintain a conversation with a reader. In a sense, the computer can make such interaction a routine feature; and this may explain the curious addictiveness of the activity of computer programming. It is as if we were getting the normal brain reward for work that the micro-processor has done.

Out of these features comes another; the ability of the computer to generate alternate scenarios or world models, based on different variables. Now it is this activity that the human brain is supremely good at, and which constitutes our odd unspecialized specialization as animals. Compared with our own fantastic power and subtlety in this regard—consider the astonishing reality, force, and hidden wisdom in a really good dream, for instance—a computer's skills are crude and clumsy. But we have never before had such help as it can offer. In the realm of the numerical, especially the iterative and the recursive, where the result of an equation can be fed back into the equation a million times over, and then represented visually in the exquisite patterns of the Mandelbrot Set or Conway's Game of Life, the computer offers to us a whole new set of senses. This dynamic reflexiveness may be the most unique capacity that the computer offers to the academy.

Our internal world models, as I hinted earlier, are no longer as irrelevant to reality as they seemed under the world-view of nineteenth-century determinism. How we interpret the world depends on our available models of it; and the world itself gives different answers according to the different world-models behind the questions we ask of it. If our model is a universe of particles, it gives us particle answers: if our model is a wave universe, it gives us waves. The worlds of mind and matter are not divided; and the computer, as a mental prosthesis and as a modelling tool, is both an example and a facilitator of their essential unity.

Finally, the computer offers a connection with one of the great adventures of the human mind and imagination: the

creation of artificial intelligence. I believe the goal of that enterprise to be possible, but oddly unimportant compared with the
intellectual riches that will fall out from the process of its realization. After all, a man and a woman can in a matter of a few
pleasant hours construct a brand-new chemical computer of
enormous—indeed superfluous—power almost any time they
want, if they are prepared for the years of programming it will
require. But to trace a different path to intelligence—imagine
the wisdom and insight *that* would lead out of us. "To lead
out:" if we translate that phrase literally into Latin, we get
"educate."

# The University

## RUDOLPH J. MELONE

*Dr. Melone is
special consultant to the President of Saybrook Institute;
he is a former popular newspaper columnist and past
president of Gavilan College.*

A large corporation has recently installed a new production system. To its surprise, executives of the corporation learned that many of the firm's employees encountered difficulties understanding instructions and performing simple calculations necessary to operate the system. Soon afterwards, 22,000 employees of the company were given examinations in the basic skills of reading, writing, and arithmetic. Only 3,000 passed!

It is currently estimated that there are over thirty million functional illiterates in the United States. Every year this number increases by two million. These are people who have severe difficulty passing a driver's license written examination, cannot read a daily newspaper; these are people who, to their misfortune, cannot distinguish between a brad and a bolt when attempting to follow simple written instructions. As a result, business and industry spend over twenty-five billion dollars each year trying to educate a work force presented to them by a system of education that cannot stem the tide of functional illiteracy. Business leaders complain about this sorry statistic. Even college and university officials point to remedial English classes that exist in disgraceful proportion to their English literature classes.

Meanwhile, publishers are striving to enlarge the numbers of written works of worth and quality, and of course, to expand the number of readers of such fine works.

In the face of the shocking statistics cited above, where will these readers be found? Their potential numbers must indeed be shrinking. Note that we have mentioned the numbers of functional illiterates in this country; we have not called out the numbers of "couch potatoes" who sate themselves regularly on a diet of televised bubble gum, nor the fact that most young people have spent more hours before a television set than in a classroom by the time they have (or should have) graduated from high school.

It is terribly obvious that education in this nation needs dramatic changes. Where, however, should we start? It is not just a matter of throwing money into buildings and books, not to mention computer equipment, nor is it a case of simply, through money, reducing a high student/teacher ratio. We need to go to the heart of the matter. Who has the greatest impact on a child's desire to learn? Longitudinal studies have continuously indicated that the mother is first, the teacher a close second. My own personal creep to a conclusion, after some forty years as an educator, is that the most crucial changes need to be made in the selection and preparation of future teachers and immediate efforts to reward and redevelop the existing teacher force.

It is a shameful fact that students entering teacher preparation programs are among those who have scored lowest on college entrance exams. That needs to be turned around immediately, regardless of our desperation to replace an aging teaching force and rapidly growing numbers of children of the "baby boomlet" era. To do this, the social and financial rewards for becoming a teacher must be reasonably commensurate with those to be expected in business, engineering, medical and other well-paying professional fields. Selection and compensation, however, are not enough to improve an unfortunate situation in this country. The curriculum at most teacher preparation programs needs drastic overhaul. This is where publishers can play a major role.

Executives in the publishing industry, as well as all other persons whom they can influence, need to raise their strong voice toward the shaping of that curriculum. They need to call for more general education along with substantial amounts of reading and writing so that future teachers are more completely aware of the high quality works of worth available to them and their future students.

Maintaining a sense of wonder is critical for our teachers as they attempt to transmit the awesome ability of the human to learn from cradle to grave.

# 7 Reading And Publishing

# Reading Textbooks

## DONALD S. LAMM

*Mr. Lamm is
president and chairman of the board of W. W. Norton
& Company, Inc. and president of Liveright
Publishing Corporation and W. W. Norton & Company
Ltd., London. He is also president, Board of
Governors, Yale University Press. His contribution
is taken from a longer address delivered at
the University of Iowa where he was the
Ida H. Beam distinguished visiting lecturer in 1988.*

If the population at large is apparently reading fewer books, what is happening with that special subset, the college students?

The Vietnam War provides an all too convenient watershed for American life since mid-century. We trace changes in political attitudes back to the war; with equal benefit of hindsight, we can find the matrix of a new educational order emerging from the campus crisis of the war years. Tradition, whether manifested in the curriculum itself or in the deference accorded professors by their students or even in the unwritten collegiate dress code, was the first casualty. Amidst the upheavals of the later 1960s, the humanities were displaced from their commanding positions in courses of study. Over a period of three or four years, the percentage of students majoring in English, for example, tumbled from 14% of all full-time students to less than 1%. History and foreign languages didn't have quite so far to fall, but they too lost ground to the social sciences and eventually to vocational and professional studies. Not long after, computers burgeoned on the campus and so did the new field of computer science which at first drew jibes even from some practitioners. "Any discipline that has to call itself a science is not a science," insisted a friend of mine, himself the creator of a major programming language.

Among the changes wrought by this new educational order was the re-emergence of the textbook as the chief source of learning outside the classroom. For a few heady years in the early 1960s, teachers in fields such as history had assigned a dozen or so paperback books in lieu of the textbook. Some, of course, still do. But the greater number trimmed back their reading lists; some paperbacks survived as recommended but not required reading, the virtual kiss of death on book sales as any college store manager can tell you. As textbooks came back in strength, often for the first time in a discipline, so appeared the study guide or student workbook. A variant of Gresham's Law was at work whereby teaching materials common at the secondary school level began to have college-level analogs.

Publishers did not miss the opportunity afforded by the
new textbook emphasis. In nearly all disciplines, texts that had
been clear market leaders came under challenge not from a
single new competitor but frequently ten or more in a single
season. There were, of course, new ways to present some
fields; in biology, for example, a new textbook with an inte-
grated approach to plant and animal kingdoms stressing
evolution and genetics swept away many of the established
texts. For the greater number of the challengers were
unabashed copy cats, right down to formats. There was not a
dime's worth of difference among them in organization and
precious little in content. So began a process of product differ-
entiation, as economists term it. The textbooks of the Seventies
received the publishing equivalent of tail fins and wire wheels;
material designed to enliven a discussion was surprinted on a
color background or segregated from the running text discussion by ruled lines that created a box. Two psychologists at
Carnegie-Mellon University investigating student reading
habits disclosed their not surprising evidence that students
tended to skip over the boxed material. For students are no
slouches when it comes to short cuts. It took them little time to
figure out that copy intended to heighten their interest in the
subject was not likely to appear on an examination.

What boxes didn't accomplish, cutting down on the
words in the text, increases in illustrations did. Publishers
stressed in their advertising the "graphics," meaning pictures,
large type headings, and anything else that would break up
long passages of prose. The buzzword was "functional" illustrations. But what was functional about a photograph in a psychology text of an elderly man in a blazer sitting in a
convertible with a banner draped over the side that read
"Yale's Oldest Living Graduate"? Perhaps the illustration was
followed by a question that asked how one could tell whether
the old boy was alive.

Thus the physical book was transformed. At the same
time, certain new editorial cliches took hold in the college text-

book business. Authors were admonished to start each chapter with something from the "real world," a story that would hook students and draw them into the forbidding passages ahead. That which couldn't be softened through little narratives was made more digestible by putting so-called key concepts in boldface type, underscoring, or printing in color passages that students absolutely could expect to be tested on. The friendly publisher had virtually positioned himself next to the students, guiding their reading with a Magic Marker.

It was only a hop, skip, and jump to the slickly produced textbooks that now hold sway in the universities. The hop? Enlisting reading specialists who'd make certain that words of more than two syllables and two- or three-clause sentences were held to a bare minimum. The goal was to bring reading levels down somewhere between grades ten and twelve; the model student was not even a college freshman but an uninspired high school junior. The skip? Except in the natural and physical sciences, textbooks were shortened, often drastically. Where 250,000 words or approximately 700 printed pages, were more or less the standard for an introductory text, now 175,000 words became the target. Professors let publishers know that their students would not tolerate more than 500 pages of reading in a semester-length course. And then the jump? In field after field, textbooks broke out in full, living color. Never mind that aside from disciplines such as biology, four-color printing added nothing of instructional value and sometimes actually proved a distraction. It had to be done "to give immediacy," whatever that meant. One surmised that words, other than the highlighted definitions, were retained to serve mainly as longish captions. Time and again "production values" triumphed over content.

A not inconsiderable number of professors were unmoved by all these widely touted improvements in textbooks. Were these professors the last ditch defenders of the printed word? Not at all. Insisting that all textbooks were more or less the same, they looked to the aids that publishers provided for the instructor: at first, teacher's manuals with built-in lesson plans and tips for classroom instruction; then, printed testbanks, assemblages of canned multiple choice questions that could be mustered into service whenever time came to administer an exam or quiz; and now, far more extensive computer-based test files, with questions graded according to degrees of difficulty and cross referenced to the appropriate pages in the text. Now, for example, the publisher's package that promises the least work for the instructor rather than the textbook itself often carries the day when book selection time rolls around.

# *What Sells*

JUDITH APPELBAUM

*Judith Appelbaum,*
*formerly managing editor of* **Publishers Weekly**
*and formerly a columnist and reviewer for* **The New**
**York Times Book Review,** *is managing director of*
*Sensible Solutions, a New York City consulting firm*
*for authors and writers. She is the author of*
**How to Get Happily Published.**

If you want to know which books are among our era's bestsellers, don't look on the United States's bestseller lists. Books with the highest sales figures don't tend to show up there, which is unfortunate because any book that millions of people have read has presumably touched a cultural nerve and could, if we knew what it was, give us insights into the culture it reflects and influences.

Of course, some titles that appear on bestseller lists have actually sold in record numbers, but on the whole the lists are unreliable indicators of popular taste, for a dozen reasons.

1) *The ignorance factor.* When I was working as a columnist for *The New York Times Book Review*, I sometimes conducted informal surveys by calling booksellers around the country to ask them about aspects of their business. These were people who supplied data behind the bestseller lists, and what I found is that some of them didn't even know the basic facts. "How many titles do you stock?" I'd ask, because I wanted a context for information about the specific books we were discussing. Or, I'd ask, "What's the mix of fiction and nonfiction in your store?" Or, "Which subject categories are your customers most interested in?"

"Gee," more than one independent bookseller told me, "I guess I should know that stuff but I really don't have the vaguest idea."

Booksellers who don't know the basic facts about their businesses aren't likely to be able to provide bestseller lists with reliable information. The kind of abysmal ignorance I encountered from time to time is on the wane among booksellers today, thanks mainly to the computer, but it's not entirely gone yet.

2) *Incentives to guess.* In bookstores that haven't computerized, ranking bestsellers is a chore. Faced with customers waiting to be served, on the one hand, and confronted, on the other, with a reporter from the bestseller list asking for facts and figures, a bookseller may elect to get rid of the reporter fast by guessing which titles have sold in what numbers instead of taking the time to add up the relevant sales.

3) *The effects of ulterior motives.* Every so often, as everyone knows, bookstores obtain a huge supply of a highly hyped title only to find that readers don't want it. Given the need to stimulate sales, some booksellers may decide to classify a loser as a winner; the label "bestseller" will boost sales, they reason. Often, it does.

4) *The duplication dilemma.* Major bestseller list derive only in part from data that book retailers supply. Book wholesalers report to the lists too (and, incidentally, may fabricate facts just as retailers may, for the same reasons). But the figures wholesalers provide create an additional problem. Because wholesalers report sales to retailers rather than to readers, it's reasonable to imagine a scenario that runs something like this:

> A certain wholesaler sells certain retailers 50 copies of one of its top sellers and reports that figure to the bestseller list compilers. The retailers then manage to sell 30 copies of the book; they duly report these sales when they occur, some time later. Eventually, the retailers decide that the remaining 20 copies aren't going to sell, so they return them to the wholesaler, who resells them or destroys them or returns them to the publisher. If they are returned, the publisher may resell them or not. And so on.

Since any number of books may follow similarly tortuous routes through wholesale and retail outlets, some questions arise. For example: Is it possible to figure out (1) how many copies of the book in the example really sold; (2) which sales would have been reflected on bestseller lists; and (3) what rational relationship, if any, exists between the number of copies that really sold and the number that bestseller lists would have reflected?

5) *The selective perception problem.* When a publisher launches a book with big ads in trade publications, glossy promotional materials and a press release that promises a huge

first printing, an author tour, and a hefty ad/promo budget, everyone in the book business knows right away that the book is supposed to become a bestseller. And when the list makers call, that's one title booksellers will be sure to check on.

Conversely, when a publisher releases a book with little fanfare or none at all, booksellers have every reason to believe the book is headed for oblivion, and thus they may fail to consider it when they compile lists of their top sellers, even if its sales are impressive.

M. Scott Peck's *The Road Less Traveled* illustrates the crippling effects of small expectations. In its trade paperback edition, Dr. Peck's *New Psychology of Love, Traditional Values* and *Spiritual Growth* sold 176,000 copies in less than two years, according to Simon & Schuster's records, but booksellers didn't notice it until the S&S marketing director sent them a letter that said in part: [*The Road Less Traveled*] has been selling at legitimate bestseller levels . . . sales on this book have actually doubled yearly . . . yet it has never made the lists. Make the extra effort to keep this title a part of your bestseller displays and if genuine, report it to the lists." The letter, along with an energetic push for publicity, paid off fairly quickly, and as any bestseller list watcher knows, *The Road Less Traveled* became a fixture on the trade paperback rosters. But many other sleepers never get noticed.

6) *Omission of significant sales.* Since bestseller lists are designed to reflect one week's worth of sales by selected retailers and wholesalers, the lists ignore books that are sold through book clubs; they ignore books that are sold through other mail order operations; they ignore books that are sold to libraries, and, for the most part, they ignore books that are sold through health food stores or sporting goods stores or workshop programs or any other outlet that the trade calls "nontraditional," even though figures for mail order sales and institutional sales and nontraditional sales of certain titles can be huge.

7) *Too-tight time frames.* The fact that bestseller lists generally derive from one week's sales figures obviously means that

the lists have to highlight books that sell fast and that they must fail to recognize books that reach a great many readers over more extended periods of time than seven days.

*I'm OK, You're OK* still hadn't made a bestseller list by the time it had sold a million copies in hardcover; and many other titles have sold far better over the years than many or most of the bestsellers you'll see in Sunday's paper.

8) *Tardiness.* Even if we forget about the slow starters and the books that really reach the biggest audiences because they keep selling over time and even if we assume for a moment that one week's sales are a reasonable measure of success, time factors still cause major flaws in bestseller rankings.

Consider the list you'll see this coming weekend. Since weekly publications generally go to press a week or a week and a half before their cover dates, the information it's based on is two to three weeks old by the time it appears in cold print. Thus, this week's bestsellers are really last week's best-sellers or two-weeks-ago's bestsellers.

9) *Changeable competition.* It's relatively easy to get on bestseller lists in some weeks and relatively hard in others, depending on the general level of book sales. In fact, as an executive of *The New York Times* once declared, "If a book comes out in a period of the year when sales are generally low, it can sell so many copies in one place that it makes up for sell-ing hardly any copies anywhere else."

The executive who advanced this theory was trying to explain to *Publishers Weekly* how Ed Koch's book *Mayor* hap-pened to appear on *The Times* bestseller list at a time when the publisher had shipped out only 27,000 copies of the book, all of them to booksellers in the New York metropolitan area, and how *Mayor* made it to the number one position before the book had full-scale national distribution.

Tom Peters, co-author of *In Search of Excellence*, proffered a different explanation. "Ah, the obvious is finally confirmed," he asserted in a letter to the editor; "*The New York Times* best-seller list is a local, not a national list."

Whatever you believe about the implications of the Koch case in particular or the breadth of *The Times* bestseller survey in general, the fact remains that some books make bestseller lists during weeks when business is slow while others which rack up considerably higher sales during prime selling seasons don't manage to get on.

10) *Tie scores.* Some of the booksellers who report to bestseller lists may be able to move six or eight or a dozen or more copies a week of titles toward the top of their individual bestseller rosters, but they may not be able to sell more than one copy of each of the titles toward the bottom, in which case rankings are obviously quite arbitrary.

11) *Inconsistent criteria.* People who compile weekly bestseller lists aren't eager to talk about how many copies a book ordinarily has to sell to earn a slot, but *Publishers Weekly* does reveal its ground rules when it gets up its list of the year's bestselling titles (those lists, it's important to note, are based on figures supplied by publishers, who, like booksellers, have reasons to be less than accurate).

In the recent past, hardcover fiction that sold barely into six figures has made the annual lists while hardcover nonfiction that sold well into six figures got shut out. At the same time, all a trade paperback had to do to be listed was sell 50,000 copies while "mass market" paperbacks weren't considered bestsellers unless copies in print went over a million (the fact that mass-market publishers still maintain they can only supply in-print figures, and not sales figures, is worth pondering, by the way, and I commend it as a topic for research and analysis). The point here, of course, is that there are bestsellers and bestsellers, and that a bestseller at the low end of one category maybe quite a bit better a seller than a bestseller at the high end of some other category.

Not to mention the fact that a bestseller according to one periodical may not be a bestseller according to another. *The Weekly* and the annual *Publishers Weekly* and *The New York Times Book Review* lists don't jibe, and neither the *PW* list nor the *Times* list is the same as lists compiled by other periodicals or lists compiled by national bookstore chains.

12) *The division-by-format distortion.* Because major media divide bestsellers into format categories (ranking hardcovers separately from paperbacks and sometimes also segregating rack-sized paperbacks from larger paperbacks), the same book can appear on two or more lists at the same time. When that happens, when a particular book shows up on both the hardcover list and the paperback list of the very same periodical in the very same week, then in all likelihood the reported sales of that book that week were greater than the reported sales of any other title on that periodical's lists. *Iacocca* and *Lake Wobegon Days* are among the titles that have recently occupied two bestseller slots simultaneously. The phenomenon occurs fairly often, and each time I wonder why two other books that have sold fewer copies get the label number one bestseller.

Given this host of reasons to distrust the conventional bestseller label, we decided to round up our own group of top-selling titles. Accordingly, we ran a notice in media that serve the book trade to ask about books that have appealed to "mass markets" (as we in the book industry use the term) and that have appealed to these markets continually, over time.

Responses were not only gratifying but eye-opening. Specific findings differ from case to case but at least two related general principles emerge from the reports: (1) The world of bestsellers is far wider and more varied than traditional bestseller lists would have us believe, and therefore (2) Conclusions about the mass appeal of books should be drawn from other, wider pools of evidence.

# The Older Adult Market

MADDY KENT DYCHTWALD

*Ms. Dychtwald is
co-founder and vice president of publishing,
Age Wave, Inc.*

It's time for the publishing industry to re-evaluate some myths about growing old. There was a time that, when it came to age at least, any number over 55 implied waning energy, decreased awareness and lessened impact on the surrounding world. That's rapidly changing. What the numbers now show is a burgeoning population of older consumers that is decisive, active, and affluent, a group that controls more money and assets than any other. Here's how demographic figures look for America's over-55 population:

- People over 55 make up 25% of the population, out-numbering students in the nation's elementary and high schools, and they account for 40% of all consumer demand;
- They control 70% of the total net worth of U.S. households (nearly $7 trillion); own 77% of the country's financial assets; and control more than 80% of all funds in U.S. savings and loan institutions;
- People over 55 have more disposable income than any other age group in the United States; * This market is already the most attractive to come along since the 40s.
- As "baby boomers" age, the over-55 generation will become a still faster growing segment of the U.S. population, forming the most powerful buying block in our nation's history.

Clearly, these numbers mean significant changes ahead for writers, editors, publishers and booksellers. What was once a group of "invisible consumers" is an increasingly visible market with a great deal of purchasing power, and with definite ideas about how to use that power. To reach this market, companies will be required to modify their products and their marketing approaches to meet the needs and fancies of the over-55 consumer. For writers, editors, publishers and booksellers, that means more attention to the physical and psychological needs of an older readership. This is the generation which makes up our "nation of readers," people over 55 who make up something of a sub-nation of readers.

Recently Sears corporation conducted a series of focus groups to obtain marketing data to organize a new consumer-oriented membership organization called "Mature Outlook." The profile that emerged was of an over-55 market concerned with information in the form of books, magazines, newspapers, catalogs, and other publications. They are prime candidates for book club memberships, subscriptions and other home-based services.

While such services are attractive to older readers who are homebound, the larger picture of older Americans is a lively one: as people live longer, healthier lives, they are freer to pursue activities they've postponed, including continued education. Many older adults take the opportunity to switch careers or start new businesses. With time on their hands, mortgages and children's educations out of the way, they may seek new ways to invest income of retirement dividends. They want information to help them make such important life-change decisions.

Yet this is a group of cautious, savvy decision makers. They have the time to research purchasing choices and like to be as informed as possible about what's available in the marketplace. They are concerned with quality and reliability, and reward companies that provide such with a great deal of product loyalty.

According to the Sears study, this burgeoning market, while encompassing a wide range of attitudes, can be divided into two subgroups. One segment, composed of people who were young adults during the Depression, tend to be conservative when it comes to spending money. They want to be assured of quality, value, and long-term investment. By inference, they are more likely to buy books that are enduring: classic literature, solid bindings, collector's volumes. The other segment, those who were children during the Depression, are more open-minded when it comes to purchasing and are liable to make riskier investments if they lead to greater return. This suggests a readership that seeks current information, follows trends, and is more given to luxury and leisure-time spending, an excellent market for self-improvement, do-it-yourself, and travel publications.

Overall, this is an intelligent, demanding, and well-informed market which wants to be treated that way. Publishers must appeal to the interests of older Americans, rather than just to their age.


## Book Design and Production for the Future Market

While the above-mentioned psychological perceptions define the product needs of the future market, what of the production values for those products? Growing older is undeniably accompanied by physical changes in perception, and it is crucial that the publishing industry respond to them. Change in visual perception is the most obvious of these; the solution is less so. Large-print books have been around for a long time, but it is not enough simply to enlarge type to appeal to the older reader. Letterforms should be both higher and wider; looser kerning and greater leading also increase clarity. Serif typefaces are easier to read than sans serif. Classical faces such as Times Roman, Bodoni Book, or Century Schoolbook are good, legible choices for large-type books.

In the past, little attention was paid to the graphic quality of large-type books. Yet older readers are sensitive to aesthetic values. They appreciate crisp, high-contrast images, high-quality printing, liberal use of white space and margins (an aid to legibility), and off-white, non-glossy paper stock that offsets glare. When using color, a warmer palette of reds, yellows, pinks and browns is more easily perceived than cooler shades of blue and green.

Weight and size is another factor to consider. Heavy or oversize books are difficult to lift and transport. To compensate for additional pages necessitated by larger type, manufacturers may need to develop text papers and cover stocks (such as Tyvek) that are lightweight yet durable.

Indeed, alternatives should go beyond the traditional book. Future readers, including those who are homebound, are a prime market for electronic services. Contrary to stereotype, many older Americans are familiar with computers and can take advantage of modem-delivered news and information, books and magazines on micro-chips, and electronic reading devices, including computer programs with large-type displays. Interactive cable television programs, such as those now produced for children where viewers listen to and then discuss selected books, can make literary discussion available for readers who prefer to stay home. And aural books-on-tape will meet the needs of people with visual or physical limitations.

Awareness of its limitations and acknowledgment of its vast potential are the keys to reaching the burgeoning older adult market. This is not a population that will spend the next half-century in invisible solitude, but an impressive number of active, information-hungry adults representing a solid consumer base for the publishing industry.

# 8 Reading And The Future

# *Sagas*

## BILL HOLM

*Bill Holm's
published works include poetry, prose and music.
He is well known as the author of Prairie Days.
His latest book is Coming Home Crazy.*

The *Gilgamesh* epic, at least a thousand years older than
Homer or *Genesis*, and thus the first record of what troubled us
as humans, contains the following scene: Gilgamesh, the king,
is unhappy in his willful solitude, satisfying his sexual whims,
living a materially splendid life, and thoughtlessly brutalizing
his subjects, yet feeling a part of himself missing. One night he
wakes from a disturbing dream which he tells his mother
Ninsun, a goddess, who has power to read dream symbols:

I saw a star
Fall from the sky, and the people
Of Uruk stood around and admired it,
And I was zealous and tried to carry it away
But I was too weak and I failed.
What does it mean? I have not dreamed
Like this before.

She explains that the star symbolizes his equal—something too heavy which he will "try to lift and drive away, and
fail." This worries Gilgamesh:

But I have never failed before, he interrupted
Her, surprised himself at his anxiety.
It will be a person, she continued . . .
A companion who is your equal
In strength, a person loyal to a friend
Who will not forsake you and whom you
Will never wish to leave.

Gilgamesh thinks this over quietly, and soon after dreams
again, this time of an ax: "When I tried to lift it, I failed." She
consoles him:

This ax is a man
Who is your friend and equal.
He will come.

Enkidu comes, Gilgamesh falls from godly solitude into friendship and when Enkidu dies, falls again through grief into true humanity. The failure that so disturbs his dreams is, in fact, the longing for full consciousness as a human, and this is learned when "A man sees death in things. That is what it is to be a man." Only by failure can Gilgamesh find this wisdom, and before he does, the whole country suffers from his thoughtlessness. There is surely a lesson here, even thousands of years later, for countries that insist on denying it and being led by those who have never gone through the failure and grief necessary to see this "death in things."

I try, again and again, through literature, music, history and experience, to get at the point of failure—but I fail. Perhaps that is my point. Clear logical structures, much as I love them myself, are not so germane as the "touch of regret that comes from the heart" in understanding what I am trying to penetrate.

James Agee, in the course of spending a summer writing about some poor ignorant Alabama tenant farmers in the thirties, discovered that their small, failed lives could not quite be described by normal American power values. He calls his book about them *Let Us Now Praise Famous Men* and comes to this conclusion about the poor and failed; they are human in precisely the same manner as ourselves, and therefore bottomless. It takes him hundreds of pages of thundering prose to grab the scruff of the reader's neck, and shake him to the same conclusion. Money earned, suit brand, car model, school degree, powerful farm, big bombs, bootstrap rhetoric, make no difference. Everything the success culture takes for granted turns to fog that burns off when you put light on it. At the bottom of everything is skin; under that, blood and bone. This simple fact shocked Agee and gave him a case of the ecstasy.

Iceland also had a history of losing, both geological and political. Settled by ninth century Vikings who organized the world's first genuine Parliament, they were the only kingless Europeans, but lost that prize through their own quarrelsome squabbling.

And yet they did indeed make a great, though curiously austere, civilization. With no usable building stone, no musical instruments, no mineable metals, and a paucity of food and shelter, they built the most substantial European literature of the middle ages by using the only equipment left to them on this barren rockpile; language, not Latin, but their own beloved vernacular Icelandic.

What is the heroic subject of the greatest of that literature? Failure. *The Sturlunga Saga* chronicles with bloody detail the venial civil quarrels that led to the breakdown of political structures and ensuing loss of independence. Snorri's *Prose Edda* consisted partly of a versification manual for a kind of poetry, a few hundred years obsolete when Snorri wrote it, that no one would ever write again except as a literary exercise, and partly a history of the old Norse mythology that was by that time utterly obliterated by Christianity and forgotten in the rest of Europe. *Laxdaela Saga* records a willful woman's successive failed marriages and loves that make *Anna Karenina* or *Madame Bovary* seem by comparison cheerful. The gods themselves, in Viking mythology, were doomed to perish, and Valhalla is a temple of failure. In *Njal's Saga* (a worthy companion to Homer) almost all the main characters are swept up in a violent tide that culminates in the deliberate burning to death of Njal's whole family, including aged wife and grandchildren, inside his house. It is surely a cautionary story, designed to be told to an audience themselves afflicted with a quarrelsome nature and a taste for recrimination and revenge. The book ends in spent vengeance, and a surfeit of charred, beheaded, stabbed, chopped, impaled corpses that shames the final scenes of *Hamlet* or *Lear*. The human failure in *Njal's Saga* is of such size it attains majesty, but the gods are not blamed for any of it.

The Icelanders, by facing the drastic failures of their history and nature, created a literature that held the national ego together through 600 years of colonial domination, black plague, leprosy, volcanic eruption, and famine that by 1750 reduced this already half-starved population to half the size it had been at its settlement time. The most wretched Icelandic household had those books and read them: Gunnar, Njal, Gudrun, Egil, and Grettir were the ballast every Icelander carried through the long centuries of failure.

Nothing that is *itself* can conceivably be termed a failure by the transcendental definition. But things must acknowledge and live up to their selfness. This is fairly effortless for a horse or a cow, more difficult for a human being, and judging by the evidence of history, almost impossible for a community or a country. When it happens occasionally, as I argue that it did in the case of the Icelanders, it creates a rare wonder, a community that has eaten its own failures so completely that it has no need to be other than itself.

# Creating Readers

MORRIS BERMAN

*Dr. Berman is a
free-lance writer and cultural historian. He is the author
of numerous scholarly articles. His books include
The Reenchantment of the World, which has been
translated into a number of foreign languages,
and Coming to Our Senses, a history of the
body in Western civilization.*

A book of meaning is one that moves its readers from A to B, that somehow displaces the psyche, or that has the effect of getting the reader to jump a level of cognition or consciousness. Something happens "spiritually," for lack of a better word, and it does not necessarily require a particularly intellectual text for this to occur. One example I can give is from my childhood, viz., *The Arabian Nights*, which opened up the possibility in my mind of a secret world existing within our ordinary, visible world, accessible by means of certain signs and symbolic knowledge. (I often wonder to what extent my own book on the magical tradition, *The Reenchantment of the World*, is rooted in this early childhood experience.) Most books being published today are concerned with information, and such books basically come and go. Yet at the deepest level of the human psyche is the need for meaning; and for various reasons, this culture is not in the business of encouraging books that attempt to address this pressing need.

Such books nevertheless exist, and much discussion takes place about how to connect these books with a readership that might be interested: good PR and editorship; effective packaging, design and marketing, creation of a support network, and so on. My own concern is somewhat different: not the matter of contacting a readership, but the occasional, and very powerful, phenomenon of creating one. This is what I personally struggle with, because my own writing is not about offering a new slant on a "hot topic;" it is rather to take a topic that is virtually invisible (e.g., the disappearance of magic from modern life, or the centrality of physical experience in the creation of culture at large) and attempt to put it before the public eye. How successful I personally have been in doing this, I have no idea; but I am thinking of books that were completely unlikely candidates for any sort of popularity and yet wound up with sales in the millions because they unexpectedly plucked some sort of dormant but nevertheless universal chord in a large sector of the population. These books somehow created their own audience, and as a result (I believe), shifted the perceptual landscape, subtly altering the culture at large. Who would have imagined, for example, that a book on schizophrenia (R.D. Laing, *The Divided Self*) or Yaqui Indian sorcery (Carlos Castaneda, *The Teachings of Don Juan*) or medieval heresy (Umberto Eco, *The Name of the Rose*) would wind up on what amounts to a permanent best-seller list? This is the sort of thing I am talking about; it lends a new meaning to the term "classics," in my view. Our society could do with many more such books.

# A Peril to Identity

JOSE ORTEGA Y GASSET
*Ideas sobre la novela,* 1925

Let us observe ourselves at the moment we finish reading a great novel. It seems to us as if we are emerging from another existence, that we have escaped from a world out of communication with our authentic world. This lack of communication is shown by the fact that transition from one to another is imperceptible. An instant ago we found ourselves in Parma with Count Mosca, Clélia, and Fabrice; we were living with them, immersed in their air, their space, their time. Now suddenly, without any intermission, we find ourselves in our chamber, in our city, in our date; already our habitual preoccupations begin to awaken at the nerve ends. There is, of course, an interval of indecision, of uncertainty. Perhaps a brusque wing stroke of memory will suddenly submerge us again in the universe of the novel, and then with an effort, as if struggling in a liquid element, we try to swim to the shore of our own existence. If someone should observe us then, he would see the dilation of eyelids which characterizes those who have been shipwrecked.

167

# The Future of Books

KATHY KEETON

*Kathy Keeton,*
*president of* **OMNI** *magazine, is one of the*
*highest paid women executives in the world.*
**OMNI** *is the world's leading consumer-science*
*magazine. Ms. Keeton has been selected*
*"Outstanding Woman in Publishing."*

For most of us, our first visit to another world comes not through the wonder of television or the joy of travel, but through the simple pleasure of a book. They have served, and will continue to serve, as time machines capable of transporting us back to the past and far into the future.

While television and movies may grab our attention, books require that we join hands with the author and create our own view of characters and places. No one reads a book like Edgar Rice Burroughs' *Tarzan* without bringing to that classic his or her own special vision of the ape man. The appearance of a movie doesn't replace the need or desire to read; indeed, how many people are inspired to read a novel after seeing the film?

In the realm of education, textbooks will continue to be essential to the learning process. So much of the information basic to the area of science and mathematics, for example, is best imparted through textbooks which are the work of not one or two teachers, but dozens of experts in a particular field. Access to books by these professionals gives children access to the minds of these individuals.

Through books, we gain admittance to the parlors of the greatest thinkers of all time, from Aristotle to Elie Wiesel. Each time a new strain of intellectual thought enters society, or an observance is made by the psychological community, a series of books ensues, as witnessed by the plethora of books on everything from selecting a mate to coping with death. Books become our therapists, our inspiration, our friends.

Talking books, and video books, will become part of the common fare of reading. Sales for talking books for both adults and children are skyrocketing; in fact, the lost art of storytelling is found again through this medium. Futurists predict that the twenty-first century will bring us increasing amounts of leisure time and I believe, with it, the freedom to pursue what has been and will remain a favorite pastime, reading.

# Imagination
# and Information

R. PATTON HOWELL

*Dr. Howell is*
*Director of the Western Human Science Fund and*
*Chairman of the Board of **Methods, A Journal***
*for **Human Science**. His articles appear in scholarly*
*journals, magazines, and newspapers. Among his*
*published books are **Embodied Mind** and **Fully Alive**.*
*His current book is bestselling **War's End**.*

Where's the wisdom we have lost in knowledge?
Where's the knowledge we have lost in information?

T. S. Eliot

Eliot's poetry brings to mind the library of my grandfather. He lived in a small town on the frontier of West Texas. He was a poor man; the United States Civil War had kept him from no more than a few years of schooling. Yet in his library he had *The Arabian Nights*, Spenser's *Synthetic Philosophy*, the *Aeneid*, the *Iliad*, the *Odyssey* . . . His copy of the *Odyssey* was the first book I read. I was visiting him one summer in the 1920s. He would read aloud from the *Odyssey* in the evenings. In the afternoon I would take the book down by the coolness of the cucumber patch and look at the pages. Before too long I was reading, being blown by the winds of that "wine dark sea."

I still have his *Odyssey*. I like to hold it in my hands. The binding and paper are still in good shape. The weight, the feel, the smell bring back imagined Greek experiences as vivid today as they were to me almost 70 years ago.

My grandfather's books had been shipped from England. Their acquisition must have represented a considerable sacrifice for the family. What were the values which guided their selection? They had not chosen information books or books about how to succeed. Their choices were books of enchantment, magic doors opening to new ways of thinking and to secret inner worlds of people and places far beyond the empty plains of Texas. Reading these books, my grandfather learned to internalize their words. Through them he discovered inner experiences expanding within, deepening and enriching him as he grew to become a wise old man.

Let me list the kinds of books in his small library: fiction, imaginative history, biography, human science, philosophy. These kinds of books are consciousness altering substances. They all involve the creation of interior images and feelings. They are an interaction of author and readers to create an inner reality within the readers' minds.

These are imagination books. They are the sign of the Gutenberg Revolution which became evident in the 1600s as an explosion of reading. It was caused by a mental epidemic. People became so caught up in a mad fever of imagination that they would greedily consume a book a day. Gutenberg's technology of movable type satisfied a new mental need growing from what Dr. Sperry in Part Three called, ". . . an explosive advance in evolution on this globe far beyond anything known before, including the emergence of the living cell."

This evolution was tracked by and found its expression in imaginative reading. A new kind of reality was born, an inter-subjective reality which lived in the spaces between writer and reader and between reader and reader.

At the time of my boyhood in the 20s, publication of imagination books in the United States was about 5,000 titles per year out of 10,000 total titles. Today, publication of imagination books is still about 5,000 titles per year. There has been no significant increase during the last 70 years.

However, during the same time the total number of titles sold has increased from 10,000 per year to over 50,000 per year. If there are still only 5,000 imagination titles published per year, what are the other 45,000 titles? They are largely information books. These include technical, professional, sports and reference works along with textbooks and workbooks. I am also including how-to-books in the sense that rules of procedure are information. For instance, we have cookbooks with rules for preparing irresistible dishes and dieting books with rules for resisting them.

Two thousand years ago there was a popular Greek comedy named *Linos*. The protagonist of the play, Linos, makes fun of the young Hercules as he asks him to choose a book. "Look at the titles," he says. "Here are *Orpheus, Homer* . . . your choice will show your interests and your taste." Hercules chose a cookbook, a book of information.

It seems that the Gutenberg Revolution, marking a mental experience beyond literacy, has been overwhelmed by the Information Revolution, marking a new technology of communication. But information is reduced experience, an abstraction. The success of information books is undeniable. It is also puzzling. There are many times more people today involved in interior mental experience than there were in the 20s. They should be buying more imagination books. Imagination titles were half of the market in my boyhood. Today they have an insignificant share. So how to account for their dramatic decline? Perhaps it was a hunger for information which pushed books of interior experience out of their past share of the market. One thought is that hunger for power through information is more immediately satisfied than the hunger for power through interior mental growth. Consider the distinguishing aspects of these two different kinds of reading:

An information society actively transmits information, which is passively received. Computers rather than books are its most effective tools. The measure of this society is the accuracy of the transmission. An imagination book, on the other hand, is an interaction of *active* transmission and *active* reception. That is, an author gives birth to a method whereby the reader's imagination creates an inner reality. This is where meaning and value are born and live. The inner-created narratives of reality are never the same, but they all remain vitally consonant with each other as shared experiences. The reality of this kind of reading is interactive mental experience. Information as reduced experience remains an abstraction. When it is printed on the pages of a book, it stays there. It doesn't enter into the reader's interior mental spaces. When the reader comes back to the page, the information is still there. It is immediate to the mind. In fact mind isn't required; computers handle information better than information books do. However, the depths and heights of inner mental spaces are required to get the most from imagination books. Such a book is not bound ink-on-paper. The product exists only within the reader's mind. It is a mental product.

I can hook electrodes up to your head and show you
the changes in your brain waves when you change from
reading imagination books to books of information. These
brain wave changes indicate significant differences in
mental functioning, different mental realities.

We fail at our peril to make these distinctions between
being able to communicate information and being able to create
inner experience and commonly shared humanity through
reading. The punch line of an old Sufi story is that wisdom is
knowing the difference between the contents and the container.

As Donald Lamm so perceptively implies in Part Seven,
the tragedy of education today is that this distinction is not
being made. It has become tacitly accepted that education is
the transmission of information. A good student has merely to
flip through *Moby Dick*, for example, to pick up the names and
places necessary to make an A on the multiple choice test. But
*Moby Dick* is not about information; it is a door to Great Fish
and the dark passions of people tossed on dangerous seas. The
kind of reading for fulfillment which stretches our psyches to
enfold all humanity is being penalized while reading for information, which stretches us to "about as tall and wide as we
presently are," is being rewarded. We are failing to make the
critical distinction between container and contents.

But it isn't the "book" part of information books which is
important. Bound ink-on-paper books are only stopgap ways
of communicating information. Video tapes and computer-
based electronic transmissions are much more efficient.
Publishers are already beginning to utilize these new and
better ways of communicating information. What we will see
appearing are "Infomarts," centers for electronic and video
transmission of information.

I can imagine a time, perhaps in this decade, when
"books" of information, comprising most of the titles published,
will have changed to their proper electronic environment. In that
exciting future world of publishing, perhaps large conglomer-

ated publishers will shift much of their output to "Infomarts." And perhaps large bookstores will become "Infomarts." As Prince Albert's glitzy Crystal Palace ushered in the Industrial Revolution, so glitzy "Infomarts" are ushering in the Information Revolution. That revolution promises to leave room for a Second Gutenberg Revolution of imaginative reading.

Imagination books can then find their way to smaller bookstores specializing only in mental wares. Imagine nooks with tables and chairs, perhaps a pot of coffee or tea. A new world of interactive mind will be discovered there. Without pressure from the information market, imagination books will begin to expand into their own new market place.

As information becomes electronic, a new world is coming for imagination books, a world no one has spoken for, a new ferment of writers and readers, children growing up in a culture that will expand their minds before they become stuffed with undigested information.

Through imaginative reading, increasing numbers of people have died a thousand deaths, lived a thousand lives; in France we have been miserable with *Les Miserables* and magnified with Montaigne. We have experienced *War and Peace* in Russia and have had *Great Expectations* in Great Britain. This common inner space is so pervasive that it is like breathing—we are hardly aware of it. Nevertheless, imaginative reading cuts through ideologies and nations, and it is saving us all. We've had Dachau and gulags; what is hardly noticeable amid the noise of modern politics and the polarization of ideas is the quietly growing network of ordinary people internalizing experience.

The Information Revolution will make it possible for us to seed the stars. We had better think about that. We need the intimacy of the Second Gutenberg Revolution—of small bookstores and schools devoted to inner growth. Reading is the most intimate act. It is the way to the interactive creation of common interior reality. It is what we were made for.